A Fight to the Better End

Albert Ruscito

A FIGHT TO THE
BETTER END

G. BRIAN JONES, Ph.D.
LINDA PHILLIPS-JONES, Ph.D.

VICTOR BOOKS®

A DIVISION OF SCRIPTURE PRESS PUBLICATIONS INC.
USA CANADA ENGLAND

Recommended Dewey Decimal Classification: 158.2
Suggested Subject Headings: APPLIED PSYCHOLOGY: INTERPERSONAL RELATIONS

Library of Congress Catalog Card Number: 88-62855
ISBN: 0-89693-645-7

CONTENTS

*We dedicate this book to
the many family members
(blood and spiritual),
friends, and adversaries
who've increased our
thirst for more principled
negotiations and removed
our desire for unconditional
surrender—ours or
theirs.*

PREFACE

As we were growing up, we struggled with conflicts of all kinds. Many of these fights led to bitter ends. Sometimes we came on too strong, winning battles but wounding relationships in the process. Other times, we felt intimidated by individuals more skilled than we were at negotiating and settling conflicts.

Yet other times, we ignored conflicts, hoping they'd go away and cheering because sometimes they did. The times when we were reasonably successful at settlements, we attributed it to luck or good fortune.

Conflict over Conflict

Like most kids, we absorbed a lot of rules to live by. As we look back, quite a few of these informal and formal lessons had to do with resolving conflicts. We watched our parents, grandparents, teachers, and friends handle disagreements. We learned the Golden Rule. We were reminded to turn the other cheek instead of exchanging an eye for an eye. We also learned several of the teachings of Jesus, including one that perplexed us for years: "Blessed are the meek, for they shall inherit the earth" (Matt. 5:5, RSV).

"Meek" was so passive and weak! Some of our friends added to our confusion by sarcastically injecting, "Yeah, that's the only way they'll ever get it. They'll have to inherit it!" Silently, we even agreed, because meekness as we knew it certainly hadn't worked for either of us.

In our confusion, we asked many questions. We often wondered what Jesus really meant by that statement. For example:

- Is that how we're supposed to be—passive and weak?
- Does this mean that God wants us always to be agreeable—never to challenge or disagree with anyone?
- What role should strength play—the strength we see in Jesus as well as in Esther, David, Solomon, Ruth, Paul, and others in the Bible?
- Is it wrong for us to participate in any type of interpersonal conflict?

An Approach to Conflict

Our struggles proved constructive, for they forced us to take an in-depth look at conflict resolution and negotiation. In recent years, we've concluded that the most successful approach to conflict, for Christian and non-Christian alike, is one that combines paradoxical, seemingly opposite behaviors. *What's desirable is a combination of gentleness and strength, tenderness and toughness, giving and accepting.*

We write about this approach in this book. It's an approach to conflict resolution that will:

- encourage you to be more dependent on God and less on yourself and other people;
- force you to clarify what you believe and value;
- stimulate your logical thought processes as well as your

creativity so that you develop innovative solutions to your conflicts;

■ strengthen your relationships with those people who stick with you to constructively resolve your disputes;

■ help you develop organizations that handle their internal and external conflicts in considerate but firm ways;

■ increase the probability that when you and other parties reach a settlement, you'll follow through and implement your agreements.

We think the method we present is very compatible with Christ's teaching and personal example. The approach complements the orientation of David Augsberger in *Caring Enough to Confront* (1981), one of the few works produced on conflict resolution by religious publishers. The approach builds on the process used by Roger Fisher and William Ury in their excellent book *Getting to Yes* (1983). In it, they urge "negotiators" (such as you and us) to "be hard on the problem, soft on the people."

In our efforts at facing and trying to resolve conflicts (ours as well as other people's), the two of us have had some exciting successes as well as some painful learning experiences. The painful times led us to stressful reactions in all areas of our lives—spiritually, emotionally, intellectually, physically, and socially. Through it all, we developed and fine-tuned the approach you'll learn about here—a way designed to produce much more pleasure than pain.

Resources We've Used

We derived our ideas from a variety of sources. One deep reservoir is the Bible, which offers rich examples of conflicts along with principles and standards for settling them. Our second source consists of books, articles, and research reports on the topics of negotiation and conflict resolution— ones with either a religious or a secular orientation.

The third resource is our professional activities. These include: counseling clients embroiled in conflict; conducting seminars and workshops nationally and internationally; attending training sessions presented by experts on these topics; preparing proposals and participating in contract negotiations for research, development, and consulting projects; managing grant and contract projects; founding and administering not-for-profit businesses; serving on boards, panels, and advisory committees; observing and assisting in conflicts on college and university campuses.

The final contribution stems from our personal experiences—including conflicts with each other. As we note above, these haven't always been pleasant! Nor have they invariably produced positive settlements. However, we thank God for helping us recently settle more of our conflicts than we've ever done before. We feel excited and pleased that we and our "worthy opponents" have not only achieved agreements but also gained a great deal and grown significantly through the process. We believe our evolving record qualifies us to share some of our alternatives and suggestions with you.

Purposes for Writing

We present these ideas *not* to boast about our expertise. Rather, our purpose is to sensitize you to the benefits of regarding conflict more positively and to some tools for settling it more constructively. As Fisher and Ury point out, "Conflict is a growth industry."

For you to face and handle conflict in a rational, problem-solving way, balanced with productive expression of your feelings, you need *skills.* Most people haven't had the opportunity to learn many of those skills. We like the challenge of helping you build on what you already know.

Acknowledgments

In addition to recognizing God's role in our lives, in our conflicts, and in this book, we appreciate the impact some significant people have had on us. Many of these are people with whom we've settled conflicts. Some are ones with whom we haven't settled our differences, usually because of our inabilities and hesitancies. We say "thanks" to both groups. To persons in the second group, we hereby go on record as being willing to continue negotiations!

We express deep gratitude to the many people we met in

New Zealand and China while we were on sabbatical leave researching and writing this book. Almost without exception, they were extremely friendly, open, unpretentious, and helpful. By anticipating our needs and volunteering assistance, they made short and enjoyable work of potential conflict. As a result, we only had a few opportunities to polish our conflict resolution skills with them—but they certainly taught us some useful strategies!

We're thankful for our daughters, Tracy and Laurie, who freed us from home responsibilities long enough so we could concentrate our energies on this manuscript. Their commitment to and love for us continues as a source of pleasure and comfort. We love them deeply and respect how they've hung in there through diverse disagreements with us over the years.

Ed and Sherry Wilds are friends who demonstrate not only that it's more blessed to give than receive but also that a couple can be happy doing it. We especially thank them for the warm repose they provided for part of our writing time.

Lastly, for their conceptualizing, writing, and editing assistance, we want to recognize several wonderful people. Jan and Sam Tani, Joan Gandel, Roger Edrington, Eve McAlister, and Dave Garr served as our informal "advisory panel." Their hours of reading and reacting time proved extremely helpful to us. Most of all we benefited from their prayers and encouragement. Vickie and Jack Buckman were a great help through the word-processing maze.

Our editor, Robert N. Hosack, was a delight to work with. Our rough manuscript needed his insight and polishing. He provided us with another model for how to settle disagreements in a firm but soft manner. We work best under such conditions, and we think you will too!

Brian and Linda
Grass Valley, California
1989

CHAPTER ONE

Conflict: Get to Know It— You Might Like It

So when you are offering your gift at the altar and remember that your brother holds something against you, leave your gift there at the altar and go and become reconciled to your brother; then come and offer your gift.

—*Matthew 5:23-24 (MLB)*

Opposition can sharpen your mind, increase your skill, and add zest to your life.

—*Herb Cohen*
You Can Negotiate Anything

If you're like most people, including us, you feel a degree of fear every time you face a conflict. That feeling can range from a slight pang of concern, when the conflict is only mildly important; to intense fear, when there are high, personal stakes involved that threaten your spiritual well-being, hard-earned money, reputation, or an important relationship.

Perhaps you accept Jesus' principle of becoming reconciled with people who oppose you, but the actual step of settling those disagreements (especially with reluctant or untrustworthy adversaries) is one you'd like to avoid. Cohen's notion that opposition can add zest to your life may sound preposterous!

If these are some of your thoughts, we empathize with you. Yet, we agree with the quotes that begin this chapter. Jesus' command—forgiveness as an antidote for healing the pain of damaging conflicts—will be examined in chapter 10. We will expand on Cohen's comment in this chapter.

Resolving conflicts in a way that settles matters and satisfies all parties, including God, is *not* always easy. Some of your opponents will use unfair tactics or even refuse to participate in the resolution process. Becoming good at the process takes skills and practice. In turn, those skills take time and energy to learn!

But you *can* learn resolution skills. We say this because God has helped us learn some of them, and we've taught them to many others like yourself, including people who totally dreaded conflict. You can become much better at:

- recognizing the elements of each conflict in the first place;
- recognizing the tactics which others will certainly use on you;
- analyzing the options which you and the other party could pursue;
- resolving conflicts in ways that combine strength and logic with sensitivity and fairness.
- You can learn to do this in conflicts involving yourself and another person (such as a family member or employer), or an organization (your company, school, or church), as well as in conflicts where you serve as the mediator between other people (such as your employees, friends, or children) or even between organizations. The purpose of this book is to introduce you to and help you master these skills.

Christ and Conflict Resolution

Throughout this book, we mention biblical imperatives for facing and handling conflicts. These include, among others, living in peace with each other and becoming peacemakers whenever appropriate. We believe these tasks require Christians to become capable of participating in and even leading satisfactory conflict resolution.

The birth, life, death, and resurrection of Jesus serve as the cornerstone for the Christian approach to conflict resolution. Long before Jesus' birth, Job, in his unusually graphic way, reflected the need for a mediator between himself and God. "For He is not a man as I am that I may answer Him, that we may go to court together. There is no umpire between us, who may lay His hand upon us both. Let Him remove His rod from me, and let not dread of Him terrify me. Then I would speak up and not fear Him; but I am not like that in myself" (Job 9:32-35).

The fulfillment of Job's need (as well as all people's need) is history's most spectacular illustration of mediation— Christ's intervention with God on our behalf. "For there is one God, and one mediator also between God and men, the man Christ Jesus" (1 Tim. 2:5).

The conflict looks like this: God can't accept the terms of man (sin), and man will not accept the terms of God (holiness). God's wrath is kindled by humankind's flagrant disregard for its Creator. This causes an unparalleled cosmic conflict. Paul even describes us as God's "enemies" (Rom. 5:10).

God never wanted the division and hostility to exist, since He wants to be in close relationship with His people. At the same time, from our side, to be out of touch with God is the worst of human conditions.

Jesus is the only possible solution to the impasse. Through His birth and sacrificial death on the Cross, He became the Mediator of a new "covenant" or solution. Not only is it "a better covenant" (Heb. 8:6), it's the best negotiated resolution for the "human condition", because it has as its end the best interests of both parties in the conflict— God and people.

In addition to Christ's role as mediator between us and God, His life serves as the perfect example of conflict resolution for humans here on Earth. What a powerful and exciting model for us to imitate! We draw on His examples in later chapters. This conflict, and God's solutions for it, provide the perspective for the remainder of this book.

What Conflict Is

A conflict is any disagreement over one or more "issues" or topics. The dispute can vary in emotional intensity from mild opposition to struggle and even a prolonged battle or fight. (The Korean "Conflict" was, to most people, an all-out war.) Conflict occurs when:

- Your friend suggests pizza and a movie; you prefer a French restaurant and the symphony.
- The seller is asking $100,000 for the house; your maximum is $75,000.
- You want your spouse to share deep feelings with you; he or she refuses.
- You don't smoke; your new officemate does.
- You ask your teenager to be home by eleven o'clock; he thinks (and says) that's too early.
- Half the congregation wants to move to a larger church facility; the other half prefers to stay put.
- New Zealand wants the USA to maintain its Antarctic involvement (Operation Deep Freeze); the Americans want to move their administration out of New Zealand because of the Kiwis' antinuclear stance.

A conflict can be *intrapersonal* (within you), such as when you struggle over two equally desirable or painful choices. Conflict can also be *interpersonal* (between two or more people), *intraorganizational* (within a department, company, church, or even nation), or *interorganizational* (between two or more groups).

These illustrations and definitions of conflict help to set the groundwork for our further discussion. But there are a few more facts about conflict and its resolution that we need to clarify.

Conflict can't be avoided. No matter how hard you try to bury or get around conflict, it's inevitable, and occurs every day of your life. Since we're all created with different needs and interests, every time we're in contact with others, a potential conflict brews.

We don't like the selfish implications of Roger Dawson's book title, *You Can Get Anything You Want (But You Have to Do More than Ask)* (1985). However, we agree with one of his conclusions related to avoiding conflict, "If you allow yourself to be manipulated and intimidated by other people, you can only hold yourself responsible for not getting what you want out of life" (p. 113).

Even when you have a sense of purpose and direction in your life, you still can face roadblocks capable of diverting you from fulfilling that goal. You constantly face potential and actual conflicts. Each time you request something from a person or someone makes a request of you, a potential conflict lurks. If the request is opposed, an actual conflict emerges—for which a settlement should at least be discussed and, we hope, negotiated to an acceptable conclusion. As Cohen concludes in *You Can Negotiate Anything* (1980), "Your real world is a giant negotiating table and like it or not, you're a participant. You as an individual come into conflict with others: family members, sales clerks, competitors, or entities with impressive names. . . ." (p. 15)

We strongly agree that conflict is here to stay, and it's increasing. Since you won't be able to avoid it, you need to learn the tools to handle it well.

Conflict itself is neither good nor bad. If you are experiencing conflict with another person, it isn't a moral issue. The two of you disagree, and that's merely an objective fact. Unfortunately, many parents teach that conflict in any form is wrong and even sinful. They make the error of confusing conflict with the actions of the people in the conflict.

We suggest that your conflicts are neutral, but the way in which you and the other party handle yourselves and the issues can be constructive or destructive. Your *constructive* actions can improve the situations at hand and strengthen your relationships. On the other hand, your *destructive* actions can hurt your relationship with God, distort your image of yourself, and malign the spirit of the other persons.

Lasting peace requires the settling of important, if not all, issues. When Jesus instructed us to reconcile with our brothers and sisters, He wasn't referring to a quick apology or a superficial "patching things up." We believe He meant that we should *carefully work through the issues* one by one and get agreement on their resolution once and for all.

This is the lasting peace to which David refers, "Behold, how good and how pleasant it is for brothers to dwell together in unity!" (Ps. 133:1) We assume David included sisters in this pronouncement!

Most people do a poor job of resolving conflicts. The two of us spend a great deal of time formally meeting with our counseling and workshop clients to help them resolve conflicts. As trained psychologists, we seldom turn off our observation skills "off the job." Consequently, we also spend considerable time informally observing people in public places. We actively view conflict situations in the media, and people (knowing our interests) bring examples to us.

We're acutely aware of how poorly most people handle conflicts. Even the most caring and articulate individuals put off dealing with issues until it's almost too late, or they concentrate so much on their own priorities that they ignore the feelings and needs of their opponents. Many who get through conflict discussions with some success never follow up settlements later, and so their hard work is in vain.

Benefits of Conflict and Conflict Resolution

Believe it or not, conflict as well as the process of resolving it can be valuable. It is not inherently negative. For one thing, conflict can force us to become more dependent on God and less on ourselves or other people.

We think that's a desirable goal for all of us since this is what He wants. We were actually created to depend on Him, to be "bonded" to Him. It's as if we were born with a "vacuum," a space that can only be filled by Him. The more we bond with God, the more complete we'll be, and the more He'll help us master the challenges we face. Only in that way will we experience true joy and get the most out of life. God wants that for us too.

Conflict is also beneficial because it forces us to clarify what we believe and value. Conflict produces more information, which can help with decision-making. Opposition can stimulate our thinking and lead us to creative, innovative solutions we may never produce on our own. Furthermore, conflict can get our physical and emotional juices flowing, jarring us out of boredom and smug self-satisfaction. Conflict produces quite a few benefits itself apart from any resolution.

Actually working a conflict through to a satisfying conclusion is even more valuable. If done well, you and your opponent will both have your needs met. You'll know this person or organization on a deeper level as you gain precious knowledge about your adversary's interests, values, needs, and ways of handling differences. The relationship between the two of you will be strengthened as a result of cooperatively meeting a challenge, especially if it's a difficult one. Additionally, you'll be more likely to work together in carrying out an agreement you shaped together. What's more, you won't dread the next conflict between the two of you. You might even look forward to it!

A Few Key Terms
We have already defined what we mean by conflict. Here are some additional terms to help you master the concepts and skills in this book:

- *Issue*—a potential or actual point of contention; the topic or item about which people may (or may not) disagree. All conflicts are over issues, some of which may be hidden and difficult to identify.
- *Formal conflict resolution*—the process of meeting with another person (or persons) to identify issues, negotiate differences, and agree on solutions for handling those disagreements.
- *Settlement*—the agreement reached by the parties who are negotiating; the final outcome of the discussions.

When Is the Conflict Worth Resolving?
Do you mean that every time I differ with someone I have to suffer through formal conflict resolution?
—Frustrated client

Not all conflicts require formal resolution. With many differences that are *potential* conflicts, you and the other party can resolve them informally or even "agree to disagree." This is usually easy with strangers or people you barely know because your different interests, values, and actions interfere little (if at all) with each other's ongoing activities.

With close friends, family members, and ongoing business relationships, however, it's more difficult to know when to live with individual differences and when to formally express and resolve a conflict. Here's an example to clarify what we mean.

Linda enjoys one or two cups of coffee every day; Brian doesn't drink coffee. In the beginning of our relationship, Linda wanted Brian to "just try a sip, you'll like it." Brian thought Linda should switch to juice or milk. Here was a potential conflict. Fortunately, we decided to resolve this issue informally, respect each other's different tastes, and tolerate our individual differences. In time, we actually learned to appreciate this and other differences.

If Linda began to drink so much coffee that her health suffered, spent a fortune on coffee beans and coffee-making equipment, or kept nagging Brian to try some, or if Brian criticized Linda about her coffee drinking and kept pushing substitutes, the potential conflict could escalate into one that needed formal resolution. As it was, the issue wasn't important enough to call for "formal negotiations."

We have other accepted differences. One of us loves jogging up and down hills; the other prefers running on flat land. One likes to concentrate and write for long stretches of time; the other likes short spurts and frequent breaks. In these examples, no one's needs or preferences are "better" than the other's. We've learned as a married couple and as a professional team that some differences must be accepted or resolved very quickly, sometimes *intra*personally. These aren't worth the energy of formal resolution in which the two of us sit down and negotiate a solution. You'll have to determine which differences fall into this category for you as each conflict situation arises.

Sometimes the decision about whether or not a conflict is worth discussing isn't clear to you. Consider these examples:

- A fellow employee doesn't do his agreed-upon tasks, leaving extra work for you.
- Your neighbor's usual loud swearing over the back fence might offend guests at the backyard barbecue you've planned for next week.
- Your teacher asks for class participation but consistently cuts off any discussions and seems more comfortable lecturing.

Should you speak up? Is the conflict too "trivial"? Is the situation worth formal discussion with the intent of settlement? Here's the rule of thumb we recommend: *If you feel moderately concerned or irritated as well as unnaturally tense, and will admit that the outcome is important to you, then the conflict is worth resolving formally.*

The issues in the above cases are not trivial. In fact, the situations will probably become more stressful if they aren't resolved. That means it will be up to you to initiate a discussion with the other person and to negotiate for what you and the other person both want. We show how to prepare and carry out that discussion in later chapters.

What You'll Learn as You Master This Book

This is a book for people who want to resolve their conflicts. As such, it's designed as a workbook that encourages your active participation. To practice on paper is to prepare for real problems. By reading this book and completing the chapter exercises you'll gain valuable skills in analyzing and resolving conflicts. You'll also become more adept at recognizing and, if necessary, counteracting the strategies others may use on you. Furthermore, you'll learn guidelines for coaching other people in the skills of constructive conflict resolution.

You'll enjoy the benefits of these new skills as you experience:

- increased trust in God's wisdom and timing in helping you settle conflicts;
- improved relationships based on more mutual respect and honesty;
- less fear and avoidance of challenging conflicts;

- more fun as you view conflict in a new and exciting way;
- less stress and wasted energy devoured by unresolved issues;
- more efficiency in handling difficult or complicated conflicts; and
- fewer times of being unfairly "used," intimidated, or manipulated.

We hope we've helped you resolve any intrapersonal conflict you may have had about continuing to read this book. Try the two following experiments; then go on to chapter 2.

Experiment 1: "Difficult Conflicts"
No doubt you find certain conflicts easier and less fearsome than others to resolve. Read the list of conflicts below, assuming that you've decided to formally resolve each one.

A. Rank the conflicts in order from 1 (easiest to settle) to 10 (most difficult) according to how you currently feel about your conflict resolution skills.
B. When you're finished, answer the questions that follow.

LIST OF CONFLICTS
Rank (from 1–10)

_____ You have to request a raise in pay from your boss, who is likely to resist.

_____ You don't believe your family (or roommate) is helping enough with household chores.

_____ You want to buy a used car from a notoriously "hardsell" dealer.

_____ Your employee is arriving at work late and leaving early, against company rules.

_____ You're the mediator for a conflict over child custody between a mother and father.

_____ You can't sleep because of your neighbor's loud, late parties.

_____ You're upset because a friend frequently takes the Lord's name in vain when you're out together.

_____ Your teenager refuses to go to church with you.

_____ Your roof is leaking and the insurance company is hesitating about paying for repairs and damage.

_____ Your father insists on criticizing and giving advice about your handling of finances.

C. Answer these questions:
   1. Consider the conflict that seems easiest for you to resolve. Why is it easy to settle?

   2. Now consider the conflict that seems most difficult. Why is it tough for you?

   3. Which of these ten conflicts have you handled in the past?

   4. Which would be new challenges?
D. If it seems appropriate, discuss the experiment with someone you trust.

Experiment 2: "A Past Success"

You've successfully resolved many past conflicts. Think back on some successes as you do this experiment.
A. Recall a conflict with another person (or an organization) that you handled particularly well. Describe it in a few words.

B. Answer the following questions about that successful experience:
   1. What was the conflict over?

   2. What did the other person (or organization) initially want?

   3. What did you initially want?

   4. Who suggested that the conflict be resolved?

   5. How did you feel before, during, and after the discussion?

6. What were at least two benefits that came out of this experience?

7. What frustrations, if any, did you have with that conflict resolution process?

CHAPTER TWO

What Started This Conflict Anyway?

Sometimes when we disagree with each other, our words flow so fast and our feelings get so varied that our intensity scares us. What's even more frightening is that those are the times when we quickly lose track of what caused the disagreement in the first place. Talk about being confused!

—Perplexed negotiator-in-training

In chapter 1 we conclude that conflicts are inevitable in your life. Why? We believe it's because of the myriad ways you differ from others.

Most of those individual differences are stimulating and keep your life and relationships interesting. At the same time, some of your unique characteristics can be challenging or even downright irritating to people who cross your path. This results in conflict.

We'd like to introduce some causes of personal conflict, then show how some of these same causes can lead to conflict within and between organizations. We're convinced that by knowing the various causes contributing to disputes, you can take a first step toward being a more highly skilled conflict resolver.

Some readers want many examples of conflict so they can sharpen their "detection" skills. If you're satisfied with your competence in this area, simply note the types of causes listed, read the summary paragraphs, and focus on the two experiments at the end of this chapter.

Personal Conflict due to Different Perceptions

Perceptions are your views and impressions of reality—how you see, hear, smell, and otherwise sense the world. All of us perceive objects and situations uniquely. What you observe may be very different from what your neighbor sees and hears.

You can even have conflicting perceptions of yourself. This *intrapersonal* conflict results when you perceive something about yourself in at least two different, contradictory ways. For example:

- When you look into a full-length mirror, you see certain parts of your body as relatively attractive and other parts as disappointing. As a result, you have conflicting impressions of your physical qualities.

- You struggle over whether or not you'll go to heaven when you die. You know you've accepted Jesus Christ as your Saviour, but you perceive your past, or even your present, as so unworthy that you doubt you'll really make it.

Interpersonal conflicts due to different perceptions are a little easier to illustrate. People simply see the same things differently. This seems natural, but it creates so much pain! Can you add a couple of your recent perception-caused conflicts to these two examples?

- You and your sibling see your father in a very different light. You see him as attentive and involved with all your family members. The other regards him as showing favoritism, primarily to you.

- Your boss is less than pleased with the artwork you just produced. You think it is one of the more creative and provocative covers you've ever submitted. Hesitantly, he tells you it's trite and "too loose." He even hints that you didn't spend enough time on it.

Even when you know that the source of a conflict is opposite perceptions, you might have to dig further to discover more basic causes of the conflict. Perceptual differences usually result from differences in beliefs, feelings, and values.

Personal Conflict due to Different Beliefs

Not only can you perceive your world differently than someone else, but you can have different, perhaps opposing, beliefs about it. Your beliefs are the generalizations you draw, usually after repeated experiences. Only after you observe something regularly occurring do you trust your perceptions enough to form an opinion about it. Here are some more examples of opposing beliefs, this time resulting in internal conflict:

- Your "self talk" (what you say to yourself about yourself) tends to end up in conflict. In certain situations, you're quite confident and tell yourself so. But at other times, negative thoughts such as "I can't do it!" and "I'm not ready for this" conflict with your productive beliefs.

- Your thoughts about God cause you great concern. You enjoy believing He's your Heavenly Father who deeply cares about you. But you also believe He wants respect and can get angry. As a result, you experience a conflict over how you should relate to Him.

Following are two interpersonal conflict examples based on opposing expectations:

- You're assigned to work for three months in the People's Republic of China. Because of what you've heard and read about Communism, you expect the Chinese to be unfriendly, distant, concerned only about the group, and even antagonistic to foreigners.

  Your hosts expect you to be an aggressive capitalist who knows little about their country, cares only for comfort and materialism, and isn't interested in China's development. As you meet each other for the first time, you both expect big problems.

■ Your wife expects you to help with the cleanup after parties in your home. Invariably, you're tired from your great performance as the affable host. Deep down you're convinced these chores are part of her job description. She believes, just as intensely, that this is a shared job.

Conflict due to Different Feelings

Intense disagreements are aggravated more often by feelings than they are by the perceptual or belief factors we describe above. Feelings are the emotional or affective reactions you have about what you observe (perceptions) and think (beliefs). In our book *Men Have Feelings, Too!* (1988), we list examples of the wide range of feelings you can have—either energizing feelings or energy-draining ones. We also advance the theory that for each feeling you experience, you'll have at least one physical body sensation. For example, your muscles start to tighten when you're getting angry.

Ambivalent feelings in opposition to each other are recurrent sources of *intrapersonal* conflict, as you can see in this illustration:

■ You're excited about the invitation to be the speaker at a breakfast next month. At the same time you're happy about the opportunity, you're nervous about speaking to groups. You're also afraid you'll have to spend more time in preparing your presentation than you'll have available.

Feelings can also contribute to *interpersonal* conflicts:

■ You're excited about the upcoming vacation that you're spending with a friend. Your heart is set on Hawaii; she hates the crowds and commercialism of the islands and much prefers backpacking in the Grand Tetons.

Personal Conflict due to Different Values

Feelings are good clues for determining your *values*—the things of life that are most important to you. (What you value is based on is your perceptions, beliefs, and feelings.) You have many beliefs which don't have a dramatic influence on your life, but other ones do. Those are the ones you'll consider "standing up" for. They represent what you value—ones for which you hold one or more intense (usually energizing) feelings.

Since our values are so vital to us, they're rich (and painful!) sources of internal and *interpersonal* conflicts. For example:

■ You're greatly concerned about overpopulation in such countries as India. You think birth control should be enforced; you also value people having free choice. These opposing values produce an internal conflict.

■ You appreciate when other people comment about how honest and open you are. You're bothered by the fact that each year in filling out your income tax return, you gloss over and "round off" some of your financial details. Inside, you struggle over your outside image and another value—trying to save money.

In similar ways, values can be another source of struggle between you and other people.

■ How dare New Zealanders declare themselves a nuclear-free country! They don't seem to value their friendships with France and the U.S.

Personal Conflict due to Different Interests, Needs, and Goals

You build on your perceptions, beliefs, feelings and values to make little or big decisions for your life. Some of the bigger choices you'll make that will influence how you'll live on this planet and where you'll spend eternity involve selecting your interests, determining your needs and desires, and selecting your goals. More specifically, your:

■ *interests* are the activities you most like to do (singing, golfing, reading detective novels);

■ *needs and desires* are the gaps and areas for improvement you see in your life (to improve your tennis game, to make more friends, to sing on key more often); and

■ *measurable goals* are statements of the improvements you choose to set for your *career* (to apply for at least eight marketing director jobs over the next three months) and *personal life* (to land a solo singing spot).

Your interests, needs, and goals are important elements in

determining how productive and satisfying your life is now and will be in the future. However, they don't always mesh well. Arguments can result within yourself or between you and other people. Here's an *intrapersonal* example:

■ Your two most important needs right now are to get a better job, and to deepen your friendships. It appears you'll have to move to another city to get the career change you want. That means leaving the few good friendships you already have plus the ones you've just started to cultivate. And you'll have to start all over in a new place!

■ The year is flying by! You can't find the time and energy to work on both your job search and your goal to land a solo singing role. Something has to give.

No less challenging are social or *interpersonal* conflicts based on differing interests, needs, and goals.

■ Your singing in the choir keeps you away from your spouse and children a fourth night each week. You've tried unsuccessfully to get them to join the choir with you, but singing doesn't interest them.

■ Your minister is disappointed in hearing that you might move to another city to get the job you want. He asks you to remember the important role you play in your church's singles' program. His dissatisfaction with your decision and need for your help injects gray clouds into your new career horizon.

Personal Conflict due to Different Behavior Patterns
All the ingredients we've discussed so far in this chapter influence ways you act or behave. Your outward (overt) behaviors and habit patterns can be observed by other people. In turn, your different behavior patterns are the most obvious source of personal conflict since they're based on observable actions. Your actions can be at odds with each other as well as with those of people with whom you come in contact. Think of times when you had conflicts within yourself because of this. Here's an example to stimulate your thinking:

■ You value daily devotional time—reading Scripture,

meditating on thoughts from a devotional book, and praying. When you do it, you feel closer to God and more centered throughout that day. But somehow it's easy for you to procrastinate. You get busy attacking other highly necessary chores, and then you're too late or tired for time with God. In those cases, you definitely feel a sense of loss, but that doesn't help you to be more disciplined. For us, being divided against ourselves is more painful than having unresolved conflict with other people we care about!

Here is a vignette of *interpersonal* conflict stemming from opposing behavior patterns:

■ Although you dislike disagreeing with other members of a committee you're on, you usually hang in there, want to discuss issues, and try to settle them. That's not a comfortable behavior for at least three other members. They grow very quiet and prefer to wait until the discussion switches to a topic where there's more agreement.

Causes of Personal Conflicts—A Summary

We've presented six sources of *intrapersonal* and *interpersonal* conflict. All stem from individual differences that can easily contradict one another. Conflicts result when we run into opposing perceptions, beliefs, feelings, values, interests, or behavior patterns.

Little wonder that conflict is inevitable. It's amazing that we ever feel "together," are able to get along, and get things done! We hope that our illustrations, and the ones you mentally added, help you appreciate the complexity of conflicts—and why it's so vital for you to master a good approach for analyzing and handling them.

Now that you have a grasp of what causes personal conflicts, take a look at what lies behind conflict within and between organizations. Below are brief examples of some of the conflicts we've seen in or between nonprofit organizations, profit-making businesses, and countries.

An "organization" is made up of groups of people who are supposed to work together toward the alliance's goals. Because people are the managers, employees, customers, and citizens of any organization, the same sources of conflict operate in these situations as they do in *intra-* and *inter-* personal disagreements. The nature of the actual conflicts varies, but the causes can be the same.

As you review these examples, recall some organizational conflicts you've experienced or observed in the lives of your family or friends. Not every type of organizational conflict is illustrated, so see if you can identify ones that are missing.

Employee-Employee Conflict due to Different Behavior Patterns

■ You consistently outperform your fellow employees on comparable tasks. You complete more products at a higher quality level than they do. They're not happy about that—or about you. Somebody nicknames you the "ratebuster."

■ Your officemate smokes. You not only don't smoke but also react strongly to other people's smoke. Your partner refuses to change her habits.

Manager-Employee Conflict due to Different Values

■ You've managed the rehabilitation unit for seven years. In all that time, you've never had an employee quite like this one. She doesn't value initiative. If something isn't part of her job description, she won't do it. You know she's sharp enough to recognize tasks that need action, but you're convinced she'd prefer to ignore them.

■ You've liked working for your boss for the past two years. However, one of her values concerns you. In and out of staff meetings, she emphasizes strong, autocratic leadership. She prefers to make decisions on her own. You know you have some good ideas and believe strongly in joint decision-making.

Organization-Customer Conflict due to Different Expectations

■ You're selling farm equipment for which your company has a fixed price. Your potential customer assumes the cost is negotiable and gets upset when you say you can't budge from the company's price list.

Departments in Conflict due to Different Needs

■ You're on the staff of your local church. You manage the church's world missions program. The Budget and Finance Committee is struggling with some fiscal belt-tightening that's long overdue. The only problem is that their new budget calls for a 30 percent cut in your department but only a 12 percent cut in the music department.

This discrepancy causes at least two conflicts. One is between your department and the budget committee. The other is between your group and the music department.

■ Your engineering department wants more time to produce a prototype for the company's new product line. The sales department is demanding an earlier completion date—customers are waiting!

Organizations in Conflict due to Different Values

■ You're a leader of the international Greenpeace organization as it pursues an antinuclear policy and promotes the conservation of the world's natural resources. On a fact-finding trip to the Antarctic, you become alarmed at the debris and waste left by each country (including your own) participating in exploration and development activities there. The countries involved don't seem concerned.

By now, we trust that you can recognize many of the causes behind both interpersonal and organizational conflicts. Let's further explore the use of this analytical skill.

Analyzing Causes of Conflicts

As we explain later in the book, good conflict resolvers prepare very carefully for the negotiations they enter. This means paying attention to what caused the conflicts in the first place.

We encourage you to spend some time analyzing the causes of your disagreements. Is it a conflict of perceptions? Beliefs? Feelings? Values? A combination of causes? This kind of research can often uncover hidden issues and even reveal a strategy for solving the conflict.

A word of caution, however. Resist the desire to identify all possible causes of each conflict you face. You can become so compulsive about diagnosing and labeling causes that you lose precious time and energy needed for solving the conflicts. Someone once tagged it "paralysis by analysis." Also, you may become so logical, structured, and judgmental that your negotiations will be stilted, mechanical, and devoid of the emotional sensitivity needed to make you and the other person feel at ease.

Accept the fact that you'll seldom be able to identify all the underlying causes, particularly for complicated disputes. Some causes which are enmeshed heavily in both sides' behavior patterns will defy detection.

See how skillful you've become at identifying the possible causes of conflict. Try the two experiments, and check your responses with our versions at the end of the chapter.

As an example, we have provided sample answers to the following experiments. This is the only chapter where we have done so. We thought you might like to have something concrete against which to evaluate your responses and assess your skills for detecting conflict causes.

Experiment 3: "Sources of Conflict—in the Bible"
The Bible describes many conflicts between people. Look up the three conflicts described below, and complete the following:
A. For each of the conflicts, list two possible causes that produced that disagreement. Was it due to perceptions, feelings, beliefs, values, interests, or behavior patterns?
   1. Paul and Barnabas disagreed with men from Judea on an issue that later seemed to be well resolved (Acts 15:1-21).
      Cause #1:
      Cause #2:
   2. Some Pharisees argued with Jesus in a pattern that precipitated recurrent arguments with Him (Mark 8:11-13).
      Cause #1:

Cause #2:
3. Paul and Barnabas had a major dispute that led to their going separate ways (Acts 15:35-41).
Cause #1:
Cause #2:
B. Would you have handled these conflicts differently? If so, how?

Experiment 4: "Causes of Social Conflict"
Continue to polish your skill of identifying the possible causes of conflicts.
A. For each social situation described, list at least two possible sources of conflict (perceptions, beliefs, feelings, values, interests, behavior patterns).
1. Your father criticizes you for not being more successful. Sometimes he even says critical things when other people can overhear him. You'd like to talk with him about the issue.
Cause #1:
Cause #2:
2. Three of your employees work long hours each workday and even show up at the job site on weekends. You feel embarrassed when you can't be there working alongside them. You worry that they may resent you for not showing their level of commitment.
Cause #1:
Cause #2:
B. Are these conflicts similar to any you've experienced?

C. See if you can identify any additional causes of the conflicts that come to mind; then check our ideas at the end of the chapter.

Our Ideas on Sources for Experiment 3
1. Possible causes of Paul and Barnabas' conflict with the Judean men (Acts 15:1-21):
■ Opposing *beliefs*
—Judean men believed males could not be saved unless

they were circumcised in the Hebrew custom. Judean men also believed that salvation resulted from obedience to the Law.

—Paul and Barnabas believed people are saved by the grace of God through faith in Jesus Christ, not through human acts, such as circumcision. Paul and Barnabas believed that Christ's sacrifice fulfilled the ceremonial law of the Old Testament. Christ's atoning work was intended to span the breach in fellowship between God and humans. It was never intended that Old Testament law would provide salvation.

2. Possible causes of the Pharisees' conflict with Jesus (Mark 8:11-13):

■ Opposing *interests*
—The Pharisees wanted to discredit Jesus; Christ wanted to bring new life to the Pharisees. He wanted to show them the true fulfillment of the Old Testament law.

■ Ambivalent *feelings*
—The Pharisees perhaps had some appreciation and respect for Jesus, but those sentiments lay beneath feelings of jealousy of Christ's increasing popularity with the people, fear that He would replace their spiritual leadership role, and unbridled hostility. These were expressed by their attempting to trick Him at every chance they got.
—Jesus also had ambivalent feelings: concern and hope that the Pharisees would believe, but also irritation that they never seemed to get sufficient evidence of His power, repeatedly asking for more signs.

■ Opposing *behaviors*
—The Pharisees' unwillingness to listen to Jesus on this major issue is reflected by their behavior. They weren't satisfied with simply disagreeing with Jesus. This time in history wasn't characterized by religious tolerance and pluralism. Simple disagreement was insufficient. They insisted on going further by discrediting, attacking, and plotting against Him, along with constantly seeking to test Him.

—Jesus continued to tolerate their behavior and to answer their challenges.

■ Opposing *values*

—The Pharisees' values were reflected in their intense efforts to do what was most important to them: destroy Jesus, maintain their own superiority, and keep their vested interests.

—Jesus knew that having His power recognized by them was not the major issue. He understood that this conflict was unsolvable, in fact, that it was all part of His Father's design. He saw the necessity of the conflict in eventually bringing on His crucifixion and resurrection. These events were essential to His mission.

3. Possible sources of the second conflict between Paul and Barnabas (Acts 15:35-41):

■ Different *perceptions, feelings,* and *behaviors*

—Paul continued to feel uncomfortable about John Mark, unable to accept and forget what he perceived as desertion on the part of their former helper.

—Barnabas, apparently, was more able to forgive and forget. He perceived John Mark as once again capable and trustworthy.

—This is exemplified by their inability to resolve the issue in any other way except agreeing to disagree and separate from each other.

Our Ideas on Sources for Experiment 4

1. Possible sources of the conflict between you and your father:

■ Opposing *beliefs* and *behaviors*

—Your father assumes that he still has the right, maybe even the obligation, to monitor you and believes that his type of "coaching" is valuable. He's probably locked into old habit patterns that he's convinced worked well in the past.

—You assume you don't need his type of criticism anymore and that he's capable of learning new habits.

■ Opposing *interests* and *feelings*

—Your father may want to be involved in your life but,

feeling left out, he knows no other way to do it. He could be jealous of you and anxious to "cut you down to size" whenever he gets the opportunity. Then again, maybe you aren't too successful at what you're doing, and he's simply telling it like it is, although in a destructive manner.

—You, on the other hand, may feel plenty of unresolved bitterness toward him for his past attempts to control you. That feeling could fuel your current irritation toward him.

2. Possible sources of the conflict between you and your employees: (Note: Based on our description, this conflict is probably only within yourself, not between you and them.)

■ *beliefs*—You're assuming they expect you to match their work schedule; that might not be true.

■ *feelings*—Your guilt feelings probably are the major source of your internal conflict. That guilt could stem from your inability to clarify your own values regarding a balance between your work and home/leisure time. Another guilt source might be that you've established your values, but you're having difficulty accepting and living by them. So now you're torn between time spent on and off the job.

Still another source could be fear. You're nervous about bringing up this issue with your employees to check it out and, if necessary, resolve any interpersonal conflict that exists.

CHAPTER THREE

Mishandling Interpersonal Conflicts—The Errors We Can Make

Do not go out hastily to argue your case; otherwise, what will you do in the end, when your neighbor puts you to shame?

—*Proverbs 25:8*

If you recently made some mistakes in resolving a conflict, then join the crowd; you're in good company! Even skilled negotiators make crucial errors now and then. Here are some actual incidents of naive negotiating.

King Herod, an experienced ruler and negotiator, was so impressed by the dancing of his stepdaughter that he, without thinking, made her a preposterous offer: "Whatever you ask me, I will give it to you up to half my kingdom" (Mark 6:22-23, MLB). To his shock and regret, she demanded the head of John the Baptist on a platter, a man whom Herod greatly respected.

Professional negotiator Roger Dawson, author of *You Can*

Get Anything You Want (1985), estimates that he paid at least $20,000 more than he should have for a house. Because he forgot to coach his family members to act nonchalantly, they enthusiastically let the seller know how badly they wanted the house. The result? The seller knew he could stick to his asking price.

The United States failed to anticipate the negotiating style of the North Vietnamese during the Paris peace talks settling the Vietnam War. Assuming the resolution would go quickly, and encouraged to wrap up discussions by the November elections, Averill Harriman booked a hotel room for two weeks near the discussion headquarters.

The North Vietnamese, on the other hand, leased a villa outside Paris for two years. Exhibiting forbearance and all the time in the world, the Vietnamese delayed the talks for weeks as they argued over the shape of the conference table. The time delays pressured the U.S. into important concessions during the negotiations.

While the two of us worked at an international research and development firm, we wrote many proposals to the U.S. federal government, several state governments, and private institutions. Some of these proposals were funded; others lost out to other, often larger, contractors.

In one federal effort that was especially important to us and to our proposed prime contractor, a Native American group, we had more than the usual difficulty guessing what the federal government would estimate as an appropriate project cost. (This figure is only hinted at in most federal requests for proposals.) Nonetheless, we came up with a figure and submitted our package.

Weeks later, the decision was narrowed down to us and one other firm. Both proposals were evaluated as acceptable. In fact, we later learned that ours was rated technically stronger. The final result: we *lost* the project to the other firm strictly because of budget. We had calculated the government's estimate to be $3,000 more than what our competitor did. We didn't trim our cost estimates as much as we should have.

The other bidder had taken the time to make a careful

study of this government agency's recent budget activities, including its funding pattern for similar projects. The government made its decision solely on the basis of this relatively small saving (the final dollar price was in the hundreds of thousands). It was a painful and lasting lesson for us on the need for better planning.

We venture to guess that each of these naive parties, including us, went out too hastily to argue their cases. They did what nearly all beginners and some seasoned veterans occasionally do—failed to complete their homework and didn't thoroughly prepare for the second, formal part of conflict settlement—the face-to-face discussions, or in our case, the written offer. They "winged it," and in most significant conflicts, such poor planning simply does not work.

In this chapter, we present twelve common poor-planning or poor-implementation errors we've observed in conflict-resolvers, particularly in those who take the lead in settling conflicts with other people. We introduce them now to sharpen your skills of analyzing what people do wrong, probably without even realizing it. Take note of these errors because some imply ways you can better handle your *intrapersonal* conflicts, not just your interpersonal or organizational ones.

1. Ignoring Conflicts That Should Be Resolved

"Things are fine." The most common error made is to deny that a conflict exists in the first place. The second most common is to avoid trying to settle these conflicts when they finally come to the surface.

Families, neighbors, office staffs, Christians and non-Christians alike often go to great lengths to avoid calling something a conflict. It's as if the word were an admission of failure—or an incurable disease.

As children, both of us experienced this denial of conflicts and refusal to tackle issues. Even when disagreements were evident, we learned:
- "It's not good manners to disagree."
- "Obedience and long-suffering are great virtues."
- "She's just that way; let it go."

■ "No problem. Everything's cool."
■ "Forget it; it's none of your business."

Conflicts, if they were directly handled at all, were settled autocratically, usually by our fathers. More often than not, people were "written off" and avoided from the day they dared to differ or disagree with our parents on some issue.

In the Old Testament, King Saul provides a good illustration of someone who refused to openly acknowledge and negotiate settlement with another person. David was proving more popular with King Saul's subjects than the king himself. Jealous and bitter, Saul continued to provide a home and job and to be polite to David—all the while he was plotting to kill him (1 Sam. 18, 19, 24, 26).

Instead of directly but sensitively confronting the opposition, most people adopt this write-them-off stance. If that's too impractical, they use one or more *indirect* ways to punish their adversaries, such as the following:

■ kidding that goes too far
■ sarcasm
■ digs and criticism
■ sabotaging their opponents' plans
■ icy silence
■ physical or emotional distance

Sometimes they'll take the punishment out on themselves through overeating, drinking, abusing drugs, or trying other destructive ways of coping with unresolved frustration—personal or social.

What are the painful results of ignoring conflict and refusing to settle it? The legacy is unresolved issues which continue to crop up in various disguises between you and your adversary. They can lead to strained and even severed relationships. Unresolved conflict can also mean personal over-stress with lasting negative side effects which encompass the whole of our being—spiritually, physically, emotionally, mentally, and socially.

2. Leaving God out of Conflict Resolution

Many people who are willing to approach conflict neglect to ask for divine guidance in settling it. Others go it alone because they think the Lord of the universe is too busy to get involved in such "trivial" matters. Some only seek God in a last-ditch effort to save their shirts and swing a settlement their way. For still many others, the idea of seeking God's help with conflict never crosses their minds.

Whatever the reason, too many individuals make the mistake of disregarding the two greatest resources they have— God's written instructions (Scripture) and direct requests to Him for help (prayer)—as they analyze conflicts, plan what to do about them, and carry out the steps to resolution.

What are the unfortunate results? People waste time and energy when failing to use tested conflict resolution methods illustrated in the Bible. They also run the risk of setting goals and pushing for agreements that are counter to what God wants for their lives. As the psalmist warns, "Unless the Lord builds the house, they labor in vain who build it" (Ps. 127:1). We think the writer is talking about more than a construction project.

3. Misreading the Real Situation

It's easy to misread or misinterpret a personal or professional conflict right at its beginning. Look at our friend Karen's situation, for example:

> Karen, a seventeen-year-old girl, decided she wanted to move out of her family's home as soon as she turned eighteen. She was afraid to bring up the issue with her parents since she knew they'd be hurt and furious. She spent several weeks worrying, talking with friends, and building her case. She got her best friends to play the role of her stern parents while she adamantly argued and defended her plan.
>
> One night after dinner, she finally decided to confront her parents. "Dad and Mom, I want to move out of the house on September 1, a week after my birthday. Before you get upset, I have several good reasons. First, . . ." She went on nervously through her list.
>
> Surprised, her father and mother looked at each other

and blurted out, "Well, of course, Dear. We always expected you to do that when you turned eighteen."

Like Karen, you may wrongly assume you're in conflict with someone when, in truth, you both want the same thing. Similarly, you may be nursing a long-standing grudge toward someone over something that one of you never actually did.

We've seen families, former friends, and even organizations embroiled in such conflicts for years over what someone supposedly said, didn't say, did, didn't do, meant, or didn't mean! No one ever stopped to ask, "What exactly are we in conflict about?"

People also make other errors as they assess the situation they face. Some expect too much from the conflict resolution process. They think that finally resolving this one issue will solve all problems and prevent any further ones from developing. In many situations, several issues must be addressed—one at a time.

Others believe they are totally fair, objective, and reasonable, while their opposing parties are the opposite. They see their task as to simply overwhelm the other side with logic and convince those adversaries of their errant thinking.

Still others waste time and energy in earnestly attempting to negotiate fairly and honestly with people who aren't interested in fair and honest negotiations. We discuss these difficult participants later in the book. Trying to resolve conflicts with unfair and unprincipled opponents is a challenge that even the pros do their best to avoid.

4. Not Knowing Your Own Feelings, Desires, and Alternatives

Can you remember a time when you were caught off guard in a discussion with someone? As you began talking, you discovered that the other person knew exactly what he or she wanted from you, and before you knew it, you agreed to go along with that request. Not until after making a commitment did you realize, "That's not what I want, not what I want at all!"

Far too often, we walk into discussions assuming we'll know what to do when "the moment" comes. After all, except for God, who knows us better than we ourselves? We expect our deepest feelings and desires to readily become apparent to us. Besides, we're confident that we'll have plenty of time during the discussion to figure out our feelings and wants. We're certain we'll know the settlement that best meets our desires when we see or hear it.

Unfortunately, discussions about conflicts seldom work that way. Emotions run high, time pressures close in, and politeness gets in the way of honesty. If you don't have a clear evaluation of the issues and at least some notion of your expectations in advance, you're likely to settle for less and end up feeling bitter or at least disappointed later.

Sometimes we make another even more basic mistake. We assume that we have no other alternative but to participate in this negotiation—even when choosing *not* to negotiate at this time, with this party, or on these issues would be better for us and, perhaps, for the other person.

For example, let's assume you're a married homemaker whose children have grown up and recently left home. You're mulling over what to do with your time when two former employers hear you might be available and phone you to come for job interviews. Surprised and quite flattered, you head downtown and soon find yourself deep in negotiations about proposed title, duties, hours, and salary. Before long, you're so anxious to land the best offer that everything starts riding on the two employers' final offers.

Stop just a moment. Do you really want either of these jobs? How do you feel about the alternatives? How do you evaluate each of them? Do you have to accept either one? Why? What about your other choices, such as:

- Looking for a third, completely different position.
- Getting a loan, going to school now, and perhaps applying for a better job later.
- Starting the business you've dreamed about for years.
- Negotiating with your spouse for more time to explore what you'd really like to do at this important juncture in your life.

In short, your best alternative may be not to negotiate with the two eager employers in this situation.

Fisher and Ury, in *Getting to Yes* (1983), stress the problems you can face when you don't know your "BATNA," the Best Alternative to a Negotiated Agreement. Your BATNA is what you'll do if the two of you can't agree on a settlement. It's the standard against which you should measure any proposed settlement. For example, let's go back to the homemaker incident we just described. Assume she really is interested in one of the final employment offers, provided the salary is at $20,000. If the employer won't settle on at least this amount, she can instead end the negotiation and choose her BATNA. Her BATNA might be going back to school full time for now so she could later request a higher salary.

You should always have a BATNA. What's more, Fisher and Ury say you should also have a "trip wire." This is like a second choice BATNA. It's another alternative that's close to, but not quite as good as, your BATNA. You "trip over" this signaling alternative as you get closer and closer to your BATNA. It helps alert you to the possibility that you may have to use your BATNA.

Not knowing and not developing a good BATNA can leave you carelessly vulnerable to the whims and pressures of the other party. If you don't take time in advance to identify your true feelings, desires, and alternatives in a situation, you can expect to be surprised, and often dissatisfied, with the final settlement.

5. Not Knowing Much about the Other Party
Most beginning negotiators don't do enough homework scouting information about the opposing side. If they plan at all, they spend the time preparing their own approach and defense, while ignoring the opposition's.

See if you can identify with any of the following common oversights. Have you entered conflict discussions without knowing the other party's:
- feelings regarding the issues at hand;
- feelings about you;

- desired outcome for the negotiation (what they'd like to walk away with);
- alternatives to coming to agreement with you (the other side's BATNA);
- style(s) of operating in conflict discussions?

The individuals we teach and coach in conflict resolution skills are often surprised to learn that *it's all right to search for such information.* Trying to find answers to the above questions strikes them as too detective-like or even unfair to the other party.

Furthermore, they ask: "Where would we get that kind of information?" "What if the other party finds out?" "How can we trust the information?" "What if it turns out to be wrong?"

Many erroneously think they know their opponents well enough already, so they don't bother with additional searching. Others are convinced, before trying, that such information is impossible to get.

Whatever their excuses, they are making an important planning mistake. Later in chapter 5, we will present some ideas for doing research prior to your negotiation meeting.

6. Lacking Skills in Conflict Resolution

Very few people we meet have taken a course or read a book on conflict resolution and negotiation. Their "training" on these subjects has been through the many trials and errors of the life experience school. Consequently, their skills are limited. A few fortunate ones received coaching by parents, teachers, or perhaps bosses, but most lack the basic skills to handle themselves well in conflicts.

Here are some of the skills which you could be missing altogether or have only partially learned. These skills counter the twelve conflict resolution errors in this chapter. In chapters 5 and 6 we offer specific suggestions for how you can learn or improve these skills . First, related to *planning* a resolution:

- Identifying the specific issues about which the two of you may agree or disagree.
- Analyzing your opponents' probable needs, feelings, and

usual style of resolving conflicts.

■ Deciding your own feelings, desires, and alternatives related to the issues.

■ Determining the range of agreement you could accept on each issue.

■ Brainstorming creative ways so that you both could benefit from this confrontation.

■ Choosing the right time and place for the encounter.

Second, related to *participating* in the discussion:

■ Listening in ways which make the other person(s) feel accepted and allow you to accurately understand his or her (their) views and desires.

■ Handling your own emotions, words, and actions as the discussion proceeds.

■ Handling anger expressed toward you.

■ Working through apparent impasses or deadlocks.

■ Getting lasting, satisfying agreements by which both sides mutually gain.

As we said earlier, these skills are difficult to master, even for the pros. Yet if you don't acquire them, you'll be seen as naive and possibly taken advantage of unfairly.

While conflict resolution isn't exactly a game, it does require skills and it does have rules, strategies, and protocol. Many people do poorly in such encounters because they don't recognize this and refuse to become more competent. We think it's appropriate to have faith in God when conflicts arise, but *faith without learning and work on your part is putting God to an unfair test.*

Moses provides a good illustration of faith combined with human effort. He and his people prayed as they anticipated entering the land of Canaan. At God's urging, however, they also sent a team who "spied out the land" in advance in order to determine exactly what they faced (Numbers 13).

7. Entering the Process Halfheartedly

■ "I don't know what you're so upset about. It's such a trivial point."

■ "All right, I'll talk about it if you insist. But we never get anything resolved."

- "Their company has great negotiators; we'll be hard-pressed to come out of that session with any concessions."
- "I guess I'll confront her tonight about the problem, but I'm not very good at expressing myself."

Much of the counseling we do with couples requires the resolution of long-standing conflicts between them. This is often a frustrating experience for us because one or both of the individuals enter the conflict resolution process halfheartedly or even unwillingly. Sometimes, the counseling is a last-chance effort to say to the world and sometimes to God, "Don't blame me—I tried everything."

In these instances, there's no real commitment to resolving issues and creating a better relationship. In fact, one or both partners have often concluded before making the counseling appointment that: (1) it's too late; (2) there's simply been too much pain (and that's irreparable); (3) the other person will never change; (4) counseling doesn't really work; or (5) I can't or don't really want to try new ways of handling conflict. Sadly, these counseling sessions and relationships are generally doomed to failure.

We've seen other examples of halfhearted efforts in organizational settings:

- An employee nervously approaches his boss for a raise, believing he doesn't stand a chance of success.
- Two cynical, long-standing adversaries agree to negotiate while privately telling their aides to expect nothing from the meetings.

Many of us help negotiations fail because we think they'll miss the mark. The other person can't be trusted. The issues are too major or simply not significant. Our position and skills are too weak. This sort of pessimistic thinking usually turns into a self-fulfilling prophecy that inevitably dooms the discussions to failure.

8. Assuming the Negotiation "Pie" Has One Size and Shape

Most beginning negotiators assume the stakes of the dispute to be obvious and limited to what the two sides identify at the start of the discussion. They think that the "pie" must be won by one side or else cut down the exact center to satisfy the two hungry competitors.

They fail to take time up front to say, "How can we creatively add some more apples and crust to this pie—additional benefits to the total package—*before* we negotiate a settlement for each of us?" Experts on conflict resolution, such as Fisher and Ury and Bazerman, state that this error is one of the most common and unfortunate ones.

This "limited pie" attitude causes both sides to choose a rigid position at the onset and then to stick to it. Each is afraid of appearing weak and losing; so the more one side argues for its position, the more deeply entrenched the other becomes in its own. Fisher and Ury call this nonflexible approach *positional negotiation* or *positional conflict resolution*.

What are the results of limited-pie thinking and positional negotiation? Both parties usually force themselves into the fighter or doormat roles. Later, they feel disappointed and often cheated by the settlements reached, and they dread any future meetings with each other.

As one moves closer to a formal meeting date, errors do not decrease, but rather their potential increases. The following two errors frequently occur as one approaches a conflict resolution meeting.

9. Choosing a Poor Time or Place to Talk
When you've finally mustered the courage to talk about the conflict you share, it's tempting to push the other person into dealing with it right here and now. In most situations, this is a strategic mistake.

Your needs, priorities, and timing aren't necessarily those of the other party. He or she may be struggling with something far more significant than your most important issue. The person could be tired, upset, hungry, sick, or in a hurry and in no mood to talk with you—especially about a sensitive topic. Or the person could be embarrassed and trying to avoid other people who might be within hearing distance. Most of us recognize this on an intellectual level, yet it's amazing how often we plunge ahead, guided by our emotions, insensitive to our opponents' needs. As a result, we end up jeopardizing what could have been a fruitful, satisfying discussion. This is a temptation that many of us fall prey to. Following are some examples of poor timing and meeting place, provided so that you may avoid similar mistakes:

- Father confronts Mother, in front of their kids, about her lack of consistent discipline.
- Church member pigeonholes minister on Sunday morning (before his sermon) to get a solution to a complicated family problem.
- Wife confronts husband, as he walks in the front door after work, about his lack of help with household chores.
- Boss criticizes employee right before the worker has to make a major executive meeting presentation.
- Friend dumps a list of gripes and requests on another who has just announced some happy, exciting news.

Do you tend to wait too long to bring up your complaints? Are you always catching people at the wrong time and place? Do you fail to allow enough time for a complete discussion? Are you allowing others to pressure you with their demands on time and locations? We're all victims of such errors. All of us could name other examples of poor timing. The right word in the wrong place or time falls on deaf ears. We bring unnecessary tension to the negotiating table when we neglect the timing and atmosphere. In so doing, we risk the chance of losing what we want.

10. Failing to Practice before the Face-to-Face Meeting

Another poor-planning error is neglecting to rehearse the discussion in advance. Many people assume that since they've thought through what they want to say, they'll be able to verbalize accurately during the meeting. They see role play as mere "play acting," only for drama students, and an unnecessary, extra step that will only waste their time or make them more nervous.

As trainers of conflict-resolvers, we know this is a mistake. Without behavioral rehearsal, which can help you improve your confidence and skills, you'll be less prepared than you could be. You could also be much less prepared than your opponent will be.

Following are two final errors that could sidetrack you as you move through the actual resolution meeting.

11. Falling Back into an "Extreme" Resolution Style

We all have a certain typical style of approaching conflicts. This is the style or approach that we learned growing up, and the one we tend to use instinctively when facing conflicts and people that are very important to us. These habitual styles tend to be reactionary and thus extreme in character. We'd like to describe these extreme styles and point out why resorting to any of them can be a strategic error in conflict resolution.

If you're an *avoider,* you tend to evade facing conflicts as long as possible—sometimes forever! You try to let time take care of the problem, waiting until your opponent changes his or her mind about the issue, moves away, or otherwise solves the dilemma. Your motto is: "I'll deal with this some other time."

While avoiding or postponing conflicts does work at times, this approach is not appropriate as a major or single conflict resolution style. As we mentioned in Error 1, ignoring the conflict does not take care of the issues. Those issues emerge in other forms and cause great frustration and irritation for others who want to settle them.

If you're an *accommodator,* your style is to please and let the other party win at all costs. Your goal is to keep peace, get the conflict over with, and keep the relationship as smooth and happy as possible. This is true even at the expense of sacrificing all of your own needs and goals. Your motto is: "You win, I lose, and that's OK."

While occasionally sacrificing your own wishes can make great sense, using this as your only approach to conflict resolution does not. You'll eventually resent yourself for being a doormat and resent others for taking advantage of you. At the same time, your opponents will usually dislike playing the "bully" role and eventually lose respect for you and themselves. In later chapters, we will show you how to use accommodation in a healthier way.

Finally, your basic style may be that of a *competer*. To you, defeating the other party and winning the argument is most important. Your motto is: "I win, you lose, whoopee!" You find yourself being very hard on the issues but also very hard on the other person. The former is commendable; the latter is not.

You may win some short-term battles and gain respect from certain people, mainly other "competers." However, you'll find that others, particularly family and friends, resent your hard line and try to avoid discussions with you on personal issues. People fear you, so they go along with your so-called agreements. But they resent your approach and may refuse to carry out their parts. In the next chapter, we show how to use assertiveness on the issues in a more positive fashion.

12. Giving Up Too Soon

The final error we want to mention could be the most common error of all—not hanging on long enough to resolve the conflict in ways that satisfy both sides. We've done this ourselves.

We've planned well, worked hard, and invested tremendous time to settle a conflict, and then given up right before the goal line. That last dose of patience and tenacity seemed to elude us—or seemed too much to ask of us. Later, we've realized that hanging on a little longer, making one more phone call, or having one more meeting would have made the difference. We know because we've seen others do this and get exactly what they wanted.

Perhaps you've made the same mistake in your own important conflicts. You may be wondering, "When is enough enough?" That's a good question and one we address later.

We hope we've opened your eyes to the mistakes you could make as you contemplate, prepare for, and carry out your interpersonal and organizational conflict resolutions. We share these potential errors not to discourage you, but to forewarn and partly forearm you for your next moves. We hope we've convinced you not to wing it or to go out too hastily and consequently be shamed by your neighbor.

In the next chapter, you'll continue your forearming process by learning the conflict resolution method featured in this book. To be sure you're ready to proceed, try the practice experiments that follow. They're designed to help you build on your experiences from the past.

Experiment 5: "Your Past Errors"

Think of a conflict you tried to resolve which did not turn out as planned.

A. In the checklist below, make an X next to any planning or implementation errors you made and any errors the other party made.

B. When you've finished, answer the questions below.

CHECKLIST OF ERRORS

My Errors	Other Party's Errors	
_____	_____	1. Ignored conflict that should have been resolved.
_____	_____	2. Didn't seek God's help in the resolution process.
_____	_____	3. Misunderstood the real situation.
_____	_____	4. Didn't know own feelings, desires, and alternatives.
_____	_____	5. Didn't know much about the other party.
_____	_____	6. Lacked skills in conflict resolution.
_____	_____	7. Entered the process halfheartedly.
_____	_____	8. Assumed the "pie" was fixed.

		9. Chose poor timing or place to talk.
_____	_____	10. Didn't practice before the face-to-face meeting.
_____	_____	11. Fell back into an "extreme" resolution style.
_____	_____	12. Gave up too soon.

C. Answer these questions:
   1. How many planning errors did you make? The other party?

   2. What were the outcomes of these errors?

   3. Which of these errors could you avoid in future efforts to resolve conflicts?

Experiment 6: "Another Go at Planning"
Assume that you must replay the unsuccessful conflict resolution you analyzed in Experiment 5.
A. Based on what you now know about planning and preparing for a formal discussion with your opponent, think about what you could do differently if that same conflict occurred again.
B. To make your planning more concrete, complete the following:
   1. To be sure I recognize and don't ignore the conflict in the first place, I could:

   2. To be sure God is a key part of the process, I could:

   3. To be sure I clearly understand the situation I face, I could:

   4. To identify my own feelings, expectations, and alternatives related to this conflict, I could:

5. To identify the other party's probable feelings, desires, and options, I could:

6. To have more skills in conflict resolution, I could:

7. To be sure I enter the process wholeheartedly, I could:

8. To be sure I saw ways to make the "pie" bigger for both of us, I could:

9. To choose the right time and place, I could:

10. To be sure I practiced before the meeting, I could:

11. To be certain I didn't fall back on my "extreme" style, I could:

12. To prevent giving up too soon, I could:

C. If you feel comfortable doing it, ask an experienced negotiator to review and react to the improvements you've listed.

CHAPTER FOUR

Features of the Better End Strategy

*Again I say to you, that if two of you agree on earth
about anything that they may ask, it shall be done for them
by My Father who is in heaven.*

—*Matthew 18:19*

*The harder the conflict, the more glorious the triumph.
What we obtain too cheap, we esteem too lightly; 'tis dear-
ness only that gives everything its value. . . .*

—*Thomas Paine
The American Crisis, No. 1*

So far in this book, we've hinted at a better way—a constructive method—of settling conflicts. Now you're going to learn what this method is all about.

If you choose to, you can start resolving conflicts in ways that allow everyone involved to gain, and God to be honored, as a result of the process you use and the agreements you reach.

When the discussion is finished, you and the other person will:

■ feel like "winners";
■ feel pleased that you've been listened to and respected by each other;

- enjoy dealing with each other again;
- be determined to keep the commitments made (Dawson, 1985).

You'll accomplish this through actions that are caring, firm, gentle, constructive, accepting, and clear. Sound too good to be true? Well, it isn't, and you can learn to use such a process.

The Better End Strategy (BEST) is a way to confront issues while at the same time honoring and strengthening your relationship with the other side. The method leads to agreements which last and please all the parties involved. What's more, we believe the approach is biblically-based.

In this chapter, we present 10 key features of the approach. Although you can improve your conflict resolution skills by adopting only part of the method, we think you'll gain the most if you use the entire approach.

BEST Feature 1: Is Based on Biblical Principles

The method centers around the following principles presented in the Bible:

- We should strive to live in *peace* with ourselves and with each other.
  —"Pursue peace with all men" (Heb. 12:14).
  —Jesus came and stood in their midst, and said to them, "Peace be with you" (John 20:19).
  —"Be at peace with one another" (Mark 9:50).

As we said earlier in the book, we interpret this peace to be one that's genuine and lasting, and not an artificial or superficial patching up of differences.

- We should aim for *interdependence* in our human relationships. In doing so, we should search carefully for what's fair and right for each person, including ourselves.

  "See that no one repays another with evil for evil, but always seek after that which is good for one another and for all men" (1 Thes. 5:15).

We can achieve a healthy balance of interdependence with our friends, family members, and professional associates. To accomplish this, however, we have to express our needs in honest, caring ways. In turn, we ought to do what we can to help these important people attain what they need most.

■ We should combine *wisdom and reason* as we work on resolving differences.

"But the wisdom from above is first pure, then peaceable, gentle, reasonable, full of mercy and good fruits, unwavering, without hypocrisy" (James 3:17).

God asks us to include Him in our problem solving and to seek His wisdom (James 1:5). He also implies that we should use a process which is thoughtful, objective, and methodical.

BEST Feature 2: Requires Respectful Treatment of the People Involved

When you use the BEST, you make and act upon the assumption that the other parties involved are doing the best they can under the circumstances as they perceive them. It's very possible that they don't see other alternatives than their own, or at least they don't see other alternatives as being desirable for them. But they're operating from an honest effort to do what's right. They want to be fair and you need to respect that fact.

In the excellent book *Getting to Yes*, the authors stress the importance of being "soft on the people, hard on the issues." By soft, they mean respectful, considerate, and polite. We agree with this basic stance. We know that our adversaries are loved by God, and it's our task to try to find and remember that lovable part of each person we face— even in serious conflicts.

This respectful treatment will mean doing some or all of the following:

■ *Using a positive tone* at the beginning of the discussion ("Can we agree that we have a challenge, and we're here to find a resolution that satisfies both of us?"); and throughout the remainder of the process.

■ *Avoiding "irritators,"* or little zingers that try to make us look powerful while putting down the other party. ("I'm sure you'll see that my way is the most scriptural

and beneficial in the long run.")
- *Listening carefully* to what the other person says and doesn't say. Checking your understanding of the other's feelings and ideas by rephrasing in your own words what you heard and understood. Doing this again and again until you both truly understand each other's needs.
- *Using good manners*, including such niceties as "please," "thank you," and "excuse me."

BEST Feature 3: Demands Some Commitments from the Negotiating Parties

This feature builds on the previous one. You and your opponent are expected to make at least the following commitments as you go through the process:
- Your relationship is important and will be continued. The well-being of the relationship is as important, if not more important, than the individual issues in the conflict.
- The issues important to one side are important to both of you.
- You're willing to put in the time and effort it takes to resolve the issues.
- You're willing to exercise patience, self-control, and self-discipline as you hear out the other party and search for shared-benefit alternatives.

As you can see, we're assuming that both parties in the conflict are willing to commit to the BEST. If you find yourself negotiating with someone unwilling to make such commitments, be sure to carefully examine chapters 8 and 9 for ideas on working with uncooperative adversaries.

BEST Feature 4: Requires Careful Preparation before Meeting

In chapter 3 we point out numerous planning errors that people frequently make in negotiating their conflicts. Using the BEST, you'll avoid these errors and their consequences by carefully collecting information on most of the following:
- the possible causes of the conflict;
- the specific issues, as you see them;

- your feelings about each issue;
- the range of alternatives (as opposed to a rigid position or a single option) you're willing to consider for resolving each issue;
- your Best Alternative to a Negotiated Agreement on each issue;
- the other party's feelings toward you, BATNA, and typical conflict resolution style(s).

You'll gather this valuable information by doing your homework. Some of the many ways through which you'll collect ammunition include:

- prayer and study of Scripture;
- revaluating similar past experiences;
- thinking about your own feelings, needs, expectations, and values;
- getting advice from individuals who know you;
- interviewing individuals who have had similar negotiating experiences, perhaps even people who've negotiated with your opponent;
- reading documents (for example, reports or minutes of meetings) that can provide insights into past strategies used by your opponent or others;

Try putting yourself in the other party's shoes. What would persuade this person to try your ideas? What obstacles to resolution now seem apparent? Depending on your relationship with the other party, you could even interview him or her in advance of a formal negotiation session.

As further preparation, you need to carefully plan the timing and location of the meeting, as well as how to invite the opposition. Should you phone, write a note, or do the inviting face-to-face? We recommend that you do whatever is easiest for you, given your past history with the person. There is no one right way. Save your physical and emotional energy for the actual meeting.

BEST Feature 5: Uses a Formal Process

By "formal," we mean that the resolution meeting includes an agenda, goals, criteria on which you'll base your eventual agreements, some rules of conduct, and a written version of your final settlement—specifying who will do what by when.

If this sounds unbelievably rigid to you, please don't close your mind—not yet. We too used to think such formal steps were ridiculous, a waste of time, and a sure way to kill any spontaneity and fun in a relationship. We eventually learned that we were wrong. Through trial and error (and some training) we discovered that structure made it easier to solve our differences. That freed us up for more enjoyment than we had when constantly arguing over unresolved or half-resolved issues.

Give this idea a fair try. We challenge you to read on, see how the formal process works, and try it at least once in a conflict resolution that's important to you. Then make up your mind based on your own evidence.

The *goals* you set should include as many as three or four things you'd like to accomplish in the meeting. Keep them practical and achievable so that you can attain them and leave with the pleasure of accomplishment and closure on one or more issues. Be certain that both of you agree on the goals before you move on.

The *agenda* is simply a list of the issues to be resolved in the order they're to be addressed. Actually, your first agreement to be negotiated will be which issues to address and the order you'll follow.

The *standards* for your agreements are the objective "measuring sticks" against which the two of you can check the fairness of your agreement.

Rules can include who will talk first on each issue; what you'll do about "time-outs" (how to call for them, how many to have, and how long they should be); what will happen if either person uses an unfair practice; and the approximate length of the meeting. You can certainly add other rules that seem appropriate to your situation.

The *settlements* themselves are described in Feature 10.

BEST Feature 6: Recognizes That Feelings Are Important

Although the BEST is logical and methodical, it also recognizes that feelings are an extremely important part of the negotiation process. In fact, *if feelings are ignored or given perfunctory attention, we can almost guarantee that you and your opponent will not come to mutually satisfying and lasting agreements.*

Feelings must be recognized, named, accepted, and expressed throughout the process. In fact, feelings generally come into play before participants even realize that a conflict exists. Does the following sound familiar?

One day you feel anxious or uncomfortable about something another person has said. You aren't, however, fully aware of where your problem lies.

The more you study your feelings, the more you realize you not only feel anxious but also a little sad, irritated, and afraid about what's coming next. Based on your feelings and an analysis of your thoughts about the issue at hand, you decide a conflict does exist—and you want to resolve it soon.

Feelings are also present during the formal negotiation meeting. They are likely to have a powerful effect on you. What you and your opponent do and say will influence those feelings. Using the BEST methods, you'll deal with those feelings as you go.

This may be restricted to silently telling yourself what you're feeling and why. It may mean expressing your feelings directly to the other person in a constructive way.

It will mean accepting his or her feelings without defending yourself. We show you how to do this in chapters 5 and 6. The important point is that you must actively deal with your feelings and those of the other person. For more ideas on how to recognize and handle men's and women's feelings, see our book *Men Have Feelings, Too!* (1988).

BEST Feature 7: Focuses on Clarifying and Settling the Issues

As you'll recall from chapter 1, an issue is a *potential or actual point of contention,* an item about which the two of you may or may not disagree. In your formal meeting, you'll list each one of these issues, find out where you agree, and then work to find ways to resolve any disagreements that remain. This sounds very easy, but in fact, issues are often difficult to identify. Consider the following example.

Margie and Lorraine, who are roommates, agree they have a conflict. In Margie's opinion, Lorraine is lazy, a terrible housekeeper, and selfish, particularly when she brings home friends after ten o'clock at night. Lorraine, on the other hand, believes the conflict is about spiritual matters. She thinks Margie has pulled away from the Lord and isn't reaching out much to non-Christians. Besides that, she's convinced Margie is a little compulsive, spending too much time fussing about the house.

What exactly are the issues in their conflict? Many times, the *real issues are hidden*, and that could be the case here. For example, both women could be hurting about the lack of attention, respect, and affection they're getting from each other. One or both could feel jealous about something. Either could be struggling over a need to control the other person or the situation. Instead of recognizing these deeper issues, they may be trying to focus the conflict on something else.

On the other hand, the reasons for the conflict could be quite simple and easy to correct. At face value, the conflict seems to be over at least four issues:
- how clean to keep the house.
- assigning domestic tasks
- permissible times for having guests.
- how each is carrying out her spiritual commitment.

We might even add one more:
- How the two can share feelings and expectations with each other (before they lead to bitterness or escalate into angry attacks).

While using the BEST, you and the other party will have to spend time agreeing on what the separate issues are. This will occur individually, in advance, and at the beginning of the meeting. You will then have to write them down in understandable phrases; you may even have to negotiate the wording.

The work of clarifying issues is a tall task. However, you are commonly faced with such situations and need to develop the necessary skills. For example, here are some sample issues you might have to resolve with two types of tough negotiators, the car salesperson and the teenager. Note the details that need to be clearly listed in these everyday negotiations.

Negotiating with a Dealer over the Purchase of a New Car
■ features to be included in the car itself (color, radio, type of upholstery)
■ total price
■ rebates and other rewards for buying
■ delivery date
■ down payment
■ credit arrangement
■ warranties
■ trade-in considerations

Negotiating with Your Teenager over Rights and Responsibilities
■ hours
■ dress and grooming
■ hair length, color, style
■ chores
■ friends
■ use of family car
■ attendance at meals
■ responsibility for siblings
■ participation in church activities
■ music listened to at home
■ earning and spending money
■ jobs
■ involvement with opposite sex
■ treatment of parents, grandparents, and other family members
■ study habits and grades
■ appearance of bedroom

We could go on, but the point is that negotiation issues

take time and energy to identify and plan. We've learned from experience that these issues should be clearly listed, then taken up—probably in one meeting at a time.

BEST Feature 8: Uses a Series of Searches for Needs, Goals, and Alternate Solutions

When using the Better End Strategy, you begin a number of searches for information. Before you meet together, try to identify all the facts you can about your own needs and alternatives as well as those of the other party. Try to be as thorough as possible in your quest; keep an open mind and flexible attitude in anticipation of further information that is sure to emerge in the meeting.

Together, you and your opponent listen and probe for information that will help identify each other's needs, desires, and goals. You spend time, if necessary, searching for hidden issues.

Finally, you hunt for solutions that will meet the needs of both of you. This often means that you must become creative, enlarging the "negotiation pie" so that both of you gain things you want.

For example, let's say you and your teenager are negotiating over use of the family car. He requests permission to use the car two nights every week starting tonight; you think one night (if any) is generous enough. Instead of getting stuck haggling over whether he should use the car one night or two nights, see if the two of you can expand the "pie" a little. Here are some possibilities:

- Could shared responsibility for washing the car and checking oil, fluids, and tires be part of the negotiation?
- Is there any way some family errands requiring the car could be done by him on one of the evenings?
- Would he be willing to negotiate with his auto mechanic friend for a good price on the car's next tuneup?
- Would you and your spouse be interested in "chauffer service" on a special occasion in exchange for some driving privileges?
- How about joint responsibility for the insurance payments?

Can you see in this example how added negotiable items expanded the pie, even before the resolution of the originally proposed issue? The more creative you and your opponent can become, the more fun the negotiation will be, and the more satisfying the final agreement will be as well.

BEST Feature 9: Provides Ways around Impasses and Deadlocks

One of the strong features of the BEST is the commitment to settlements that satisfy both parties. This means that impasses and even permanent deadlocks are very rare. (Chapter 8 suggests options for dealing with these dilemmas when they do occur.) You and your partner have a large number of strategies available to help you prevent these blocks. Here are a few:

- Agreeing on criteria, standards, or fair principles that each of your agreements must satisfy. ("Our agreement will be declared fair and reasonable by an unbiased third party whom we select.")
- Postponing difficult issues until later, after you both have a chance to catch your breath, resolve easier issues, reanalyze your needs, and identify more alternatives.
- Instead of reacting defensively when attacks occur, reframing the attack as a problem to be solved. ("I can sense you are frustrated with my unwillingness to talk about my feelings on this issue. What I think we need is a strategy that will give you what you want and still give me some space when I'm not quite ready to talk.")
- Using humor (especially jokes about yourself) to break the tension.
- Conceding points which are very important to your opponent. Often these points are less important to you, so the sacrifice isn't a strain. Occasionally, the points are also very important to you, but you can still choose to concede these to your opponent.

We call this last idea "submitting with pleasure" and believe it should be a wisely used aspect of conflict resolution for Christians and non-Christians alike. We believe submitting with pleasure should be done thoughtfully with guidance from God. It should not be used to "buy" the friendship of the other person. If you do it automatically, we believe you're resorting to the extreme style we mentioned earlier—that of an "accommodator."

We use a system which might prove useful for you and your adversaries. When we disagree on an issue, we each rank, on a scale of one to ten, how strongly we feel about the issue. For example, if Brian is a nine and Linda a three, Linda typically (but not always!) submits to Brian's need. If we tie and can't agree, we look at who has to live with most of the consequences of the decision. The one with the most responsibility decides which way we go.

Using the BEST, you'll be determined to get through those impasses—even when they look impossible!

BEST Feature 10: Aims for Mutually Satisfying and Lasting Settlements

Finally, the method we propose leads to settlements that last. They last because they're the products of hard work, careful thought and research, respectful treatment of both parties, and complete resolution of the issues. Both parties know exactly what was agreed on, and because they contributed equally toward designing the agreements, they are satisfied to support them wholeheartedly.

Contrast that with the resentment we all feel and observe when settlements are based on one-sided solutions—the other's gain.

In our opinion, the most effective agreements are fairly formal and detailed. They're also written down on paper. You agree to do certain things by these dates. Your opponent agrees to do other things by those dates. You include the rewards for compliance along with the negative consequences for noncompliance. The two of you also agree to some kind of monitoring process to be sure each person delivers, and you write that down too.

Don't make the mistake of saying, "Oh, I trust you to do this." The Better End Strategy, just like the method described in Fisher and Ury's *Getting to Yes,* operates *inde-*

pendently of trust. It's too easy for all of us to forget settlement details or to take advantage of each other "just this one time." Writing down your agreements will make you accountable to yourselves, one another, the formal "contract" you've created, and to the ultimate witness of your actions—God Himself.

Now that you know the highlights of the approach, we hope you'll agree with us that it's an approach worth trying. Before you go to the next chapter and see how to implement the first part of the process with some sample conflicts, take time to complete the two experiments below.

Experiment 7: "A Look at the Better End Strategy"
A. Based on what you know now about the Better End Strategy, answer the following questions.
   1. What do you like about the strategy?

   2. What don't you like about the strategy thus far?

   3. What about the method seems most difficult to use in the conflicts you face?

   4. One of the key features of the BEST is the necessary "respectful treatment of the people involved." What *specific skills* do you think it takes to treat your opponent with respect?
      Skill 1:
      Skill 2:
      Skill 3:
B. Discuss your current thoughts about the BEST with someone who's skilled at conflict resolution.

Experiment 8: "How to Blow a Conflict"
By now, you recognize several correct things to do in conflict resolution meetings. Let's have a little fun by purposely handling some conflicts in the wrong way.
A. For the following conflict situations, be creative as you imagine the worst way you could handle each one.

1. You have to confront your teenager on how poorly she's doing in school.
   Worst location to have the discussion:

   Worst way to start off the discussion:

   Why are both approaches inadequate?

2. You want your boss to give you more responsibilities. You think he's strongly opposed to this idea.
   Worst time to present your request:

   Worst thing to do if he says, "I think you have too many responsibilities right now for your abilities."

   Why are both approaches inadequate?

3. Your minister has just asked you to take on a new volunteer assignment, which you really can't squeeze in right now.
   Worst response you could make to the request:

   Worse way to handle your feelings (frustration for being asked and guilt for saying no):

   Why are both approaches inadequate?

B. What, if anything, do all your responses say about your current approach to resolving conflicts?

C. To end on a constructive note, think of a good way to handle each of the above incidents, and discuss your ideas with someone skilled in conflict resolution skills.

CHAPTER FIVE

Resolving Conflicts, Part I—How to Begin

So they committed themselves to the will of God and re-solved to proceed.

—William Bradford
Of Plymouth Plantation

In the last chapter, you learned the key features of the Better End Strategy. Now you'll see how to use this method in getting a resolution started. As you read through the skills we present, remember that *not all of your conflicts will require such a lengthy, structured approach.* You can settle minor disputes on the spot, in a matter of moments.

But for those conflicts with great substance and high emotional stakes, you'll find this chapter a useful map as you negotiate your way through difficult territory. If you need additional help, utilize the checklist summary of the approach found in the Appendix.

To illustrate the negotiation process you'll follow, we present the following two hypothetical conflicts.

Your Sample Conflicts

Assume that you're embroiled in two important interpersonal conflicts. One is with a family member, and the other one is at work. Where could you begin to resolve these two energy-draining situations?

In both conflict examples, you'll be the one to initiate the resolution process. This will give you practice in approaching difficult situations instead of avoiding or waiting to be approached.

Personal Conflict Scenario. Assume that you're disappointed and frustrated with the relationship you have with one of your male family members, perhaps your dad. For a long time, you've tried to do and say things to express your love, care, and affection for him. Your gestures haven't been rejected, yet they're very seldom returned.

You feel tempted to give up on the relationship and settle for cool, polite distance. Yet you know that deep down, closeness and some returned affection is what you really want from him. You've hinted for more words and actions from him, but nothing has worked. He's told you that love is "an accepted thing" and that "it's not necessary for family members to go overboard on feelings."

Not only that, he has started criticizing you more often. You feel hurt and rejected and want to resolve this important conflict in a way that will satisfy both of you—if that's possible.

Professional Conflict Scenario. Your second conflict is with your boss. You're frustrated because she doesn't seem to consider the ideas and suggestions you offer for your department. She uses an autocratic style of leadership, preferring to make decisions on her own. She has an excellent reputation in your organization and no one is more dedicated or productive than she is.

You've learned a great deal from her and you'd like to stay in her group. At the same time, you feel disappointed and irritated that your talents aren't being used to their fullest. To make the problem even worse, she never gives you any feedback on your performance or your ideas. You're fairly sure she's aware of the conflict but seems to be avoiding confrontation with you. You decide to take the lead in resolving the situation with your boss.

Where Should You Begin?

In chapter 3 you learned several errors people make when they don't carefully plan how to resolve a conflict. Since you already know what not to do, let's assume you've done your homework and have come up with information on the following:

- the apparent causes of the conflict;
- what you see (and have written down) as the key issues to be resolved;
- your own feelings and the outcomes you desire from negotiating;
- one or more alternatives which sound good to you for resolving the situation;
- your BATNA (Best Alternative to a Negotiated Agreement) the two of you might come up with;
- the other party's feelings on the issues, feelings about you, desired outcomes, and BATNA;
- the other party's typical style in handling conflicts like these.

Let's take each of the conflicts you face and examine the information you've gathered.

Your side of the conflict with your father. First of all, you've tried to analyze the *cause* of the conflict. You think it's a combination of opposing beliefs (you think family members should express affection openly; he believes just the opposite) and needs (you want and need loving words and physical hugs; he apparently doesn't). You also know there's a conflict in behaviors (the two of you act very differently in this area).

To you, the key *issue* is the type and amount of affection your father shows to you. You're not sure, but other issues may be involved, such as some past unmet expectations that he had for you.

You're clear on your *feelings and perceptions*. You're frustrated, hurt, disappointed, and even a little embarrassed because you've continued to be the one showing all the care and affection. You don't think you've misread the situation because other people have observed that he withholds affection from you. You're determined to resolve the conflict and are entering into negotiations wholeheartedly.

In terms of your *needs, desired outcomes, and alternatives*, you've prayed a lot and have really given this some thought. Ideally, you'd like admission of "wrongdoing" on his part; a sincere apology; then at least two warm, loving comments plus genuine bear hugs every time you're together. What's more, you'd appreciate hearing him tell others on a regular basis how lovable you are.

If that's asking for too much, you'd settle for agreement that the distance exists, a loving comment or a hug every other time you meet, and no more remarks to other people. To be honest, you'd like his criticism to stop entirely, but you're willing to accept constructive criticism if it comes in small doses and is done in privacy. In other words, as you strategize your discussion, you have a *range of possible agreement*, not one fixed position.

Your BATNA is that minimum which you'll agree is better than what you'd have without a settlement. Since what you'll have without negotiating at all is this ongoing painful distance, you decide that even a small change in his awareness will be a worthwhile gain. That small gain will serve as your BATNA. He'll be more aware of your needs, and how he comes across to you (and others), even if he doesn't agree to anything. In other words, you won't lose much by trying this confrontation.

If he pulls back even further, or criticizes even more, as a defensive reaction to your confronting the issues, you'll at least have gained the satisfaction of knowing that you gave it your best. Furthermore, you can be confident that you are operating on biblical principles of confronting a loved one in a caring way.

The other person's side of the personal conflict. Your research on your father tells you that he:

- probably feels much less intense about this issue than you do—at least at this time;
- feels some love or affection for you since he has given you material gifts;
- will probably want (as an outcome of the negotiation) to continue interacting the same way with you and, in fact, convince you that this is the best solution;
- has, as his BATNA, pulling away from you even more or else keeping the status quo (which, in his case, is probably more attractive than your alternatives);
- usually avoids direct confrontation on issues, especially with you. The last time you were able to get him to discuss a situation, he was quite defensive and ended up attacking and criticizing you.

Nice job of doing your homework! You can see that you have your work cut out for you. At the same time, you feel confident that God will be with you in your efforts, and you feel excited about tackling a problem that has gone on long enough.

You decide to suggest a meeting this coming weekend in a place where others can't overhear your talking. You invite him to have "brunch and a heart-to-heart talk." Surprisingly, he accepts your invitation.

Now let's turn to the other conflict you've decided to tackle, the situation with your boss.

Your side of the conflict with your boss. Just as with your personal conflict, you do a good job of "sleuthing" in preparation for the formal conflict resolution meeting with your boss. Here's what you uncovered about your side.

When you analyzed the possible *cause* of the conflict, it seemed to be differing values. To you, managers should emphasize the growth of their employees and, if necessary, sacrifice some progress and profit in order to help employees learn. In your opinion, she doesn't share this value. Expediency and profit come first with her.

The main *issues,* as you see them are: (1) the way she currently makes departmental decisions and (2) her lack of feedback on your capabilities. Your *desired outcomes* are: that she'll give you some honest feedback about her views of your capability and potential and that she'll agree to try out some of your suggestions, even on a trial or pilot basis. You're more than willing to negotiate on which of her decisions she'll allow your input.

You know you *feel* frustrated and disappointed with the way your boss makes decisions without your input. You haven't imagined her responses because you've kept a log of your attempts over the past two months to give her ideas to help the department.

In each case, she has gone in completely different directions. This conflict is serious to you because it has to do with your career satisfaction and progress and, ultimately, your staying or leaving this job. You aren't entering into this confrontation halfheartedly by any means.

Your BATNA is an attractive one. You can continue the current style of interaction with her until you get a transfer to another (equally good) workgroup. This isn't a bad alternative, since you were approached recently by at least two other managers.

Your boss's side of the professional conflict. Now for a look at how she sees things. Your hunch is that the issue related to her decision-making is as important to her as it is to you. After all, this has been her approach for a long time according to coworkers who knew her in the past. On the other issue (giving you honest feedback), she may not be worried about doing it. It's possible she doesn't realize you want it, or she's been too busy to speak up. That issue seems neutral.

Regarding her *feelings for you,* you think she likes you (after all, you're still here!), and you're quite sure she likes some of your work. As busy as she is, it's a good bet that she'd rather keep you than burn up her time and energy searching for your replacement.

You're not really sure what *outcomes* she'd like from this talk. Your pessimistic side says she'd probably like to get it over as fast as possible, put off giving you feedback, and keep things exactly as they've been. Realistically, though, you think she might be open to an experiment, particularly if you let her take the lead on controlling how it goes.

Regarding her basic conflict resolution *style*, she seems to be a "competer," but in a very rational way. From observing her with other people, you've seen her convince her opponents that her way is logically the right one. In other words, she goes for the facts rather than emotions, and comes on strong.

After analyzing all of this, you decide to ask for an appointment to put things on the table and try to resolve the issues. Fortunately, the two of you have a meeting together in another city next week. You offer her a ride there and mention that you'd like to use some of your time together to discuss some issues related to your working relationship. She agrees.

Additional Prep before Your Meeting

You did it! There are two other steps you'll want to take before you have your meetings. The most important is to ask God for His continued assistance. Although we emphasize effective planning and preparation, this is not meant to diminish our reliance on God's Spirit in resolving relational differences. Our efforts are largely wasted if we don't seek the Lord first.

We suggest that you *examine your expectations* for the meeting. Be optimistic! Expect God and the two of you to accomplish a great deal. At the same time, accept the fact that this important meeting will probably only be the beginning of resolving issues with the other party.

Another step we recommend is to practice before the meetings in several ways. First of all, *picture* the meeting in your mind. Close your eyes and envision making the initial contact with the person. Imagine that you feel confident and peaceful, eager to take this important step. Your breathing is deep and regular, your posture is erect, and your head is held high. In front of you (in case you need them) are a few notes to keep you on track. Picture your seating arrangement. Observe yourself handling the meeting very well, showing respect and care for the other person yet solid commitment to the important issues that must be resolved.

Imagine the two of you coming to agreement, smiling,

shaking hands (or even hugging, if appropriate). You say to each other, "That was hard work, and yet it was very well worth it. I'm looking forward to future talks like this one!"

In addition to picturing the meeting, try *role playing* the events with someone you trust. Brief your practice partner on how to play his or her role. What is your real opponent likely to say and do? What objections is he or she likely to raise? Don't let your practice partner be too easy on you. Later, have your helper play you so you can see yet another approach.

Are you thinking, "What a time-consuming thing to do"? We agree that preparation does take time. It's tempting to wing it. Yet we're convinced that solid preparation, including practice, can make the difference in successful negotiations—particularly on the really important ones!

How to Handle D-Day: When the Meeting Begins

The BEST is based on respect for the other party, yourself, and the issues *and* on optimism that you'll be successful in coming to an agreement. Consequently, the first thing you want to do is *set a positive tone* at the onset of your meetings.

Following some small talk (very important!), here's how you could move into the "business" part of your encounter. You'll probably be a lot more casual in your approach to your family member than you will be with your boss.

A Beginning for Your Personal Conflict:
"Dad, I'm really glad you were willing to get together to talk. I care about you, and I like so many things about you and our relationship. [Give some examples.] Can we agree that it would be great to walk away from here with some things decided—and decided in a way that makes us both feel good about our talk?" [Pause for his reaction.]

A Beginning for Your Professional Conflict:
"_____, thanks for being willing to discuss some issues that have been on my mind—and apparently yours too, from what you've said. I've learned so many things

working for you. [Give a few specific examples.] And I want to continue learning from you. Can we agree to hear each other out until we're both satisfied with what's been covered, including any decisions we come up with?"

Notice that you're establishing a tone of mutual agreement and satisfaction. Neither of you will be satisfied until both of you are content with the proceedings—and the outcomes. Notice too that your professional opening is usually more formal and structured, since most bosses are used to these kinds of meetings.

Next, one of you, let's say it's you, should *suggest a process to follow*. This "agenda and rule setting" could sound like this in the personal conflict:

"Dad, since this talk is so important to me, could I suggest a game plan for us to follow?" [Wait for agreement.] I recommend we mention the different points each one of us wants to bring up. Then we could decide which ones we want to tackle and who should go first. [Wait for his concerns or agreement.]

"The only other things we might decide up front is how long we can talk today and what we could do if we run into any impasses. I know both of us can feel strongly about things, and I'd like a way that would make it easy for us to recognize and get around any of these hurdles."

In your professional conflict scenario, consider something like this:

"I recommend we make a list of the issues as we both see them and then set some goals and priorities. [Wait for agreement.] It might also help to decide how long we want to spend talking and what we should do if we run into any impasses. How does that sound?"

This organizational part of your meeting could take several minutes to carry out. Remember to keep your tone and expressions positive and encouraging. The remainder of this chapter summarizes a few key skill areas that can help make the early stages of your conflict resolution productive and satisfying.

Skill Area: Using Active Listening in Conflict Resolution

Whether you face a personal or professional conflict, use *active listening* to be certain that you really do understand the other person's point of view, needs, and feelings. Approach this skill area with genuine respect for the other person. *Active listening is powerful, and it's not to be used for selfishly manipulating the other person.*

Many excellent books and training programs on active listening are available to help you learn to listen better. Here are a few tips that will help you begin and continue your discussion.

- *Look* directly at your opponent, but avoid staring for too long at a time. Glance away now and then as you ponder a point; then return and look interested in his or her comments.
- *Lean* slightly toward the other person. As appropriate, nod your head when you agree; smile, raise your eyebrows, and otherwise say, "This is important to me too!"
- Ask some *questions,* including open-ended ones, such as:
  —"What are your concerns (or feelings) about this?"
  —"When I do such and such, what impact does it have on you?"
- Try some *statements* instead of questions:
  —"Help me understand exactly how that happens."
  —"If I were in your situation, I'd probably feel pretty irritated at me."
- Opt for *silence* now and then. Don't always jump in with your next point. Wait a few seconds, and you'll probably be rewarded with more insights and facts.
- To be certain you've really grasped your opponent's point, try to *say it back* to him or her in your own words. This is called "paraphrasing," and it tells the other person you're really listening. It also gives him or her a chance to say, "No, that's not quite what I intended

to say. I meant . . ."
■ Especially when the other party talks for several minutes, gently jump in and *summarize* the main points
you've heard. ("Let's see if I have it. You're satisfied with
x and *y*, but you'd like to see some changes on *z.*") If
you totally lose what the person said or meant, ask for a
summary.

Active listening takes considerable energy and patience.
You'll be tempted to plan what you're going to say next
instead of concentrating on your opponent's comments. But
the benefits of genuine active listening are excellent. You'll
gain at least two payoffs: better information and a negotiating partner who feels respected. Let's return to your two
conversations to demonstrate some active listening responses. First, for your personal conflict:

Dad: "I'm not sure we're going to get anywhere in this
talk. We never do."

You: "You're not sure it's going to be worth spending
this time talking. (Wait for sign of agreement.) Tell
me, Dad, what specifically do I do that turns you off
when we start having a discussion like this?"

Dad: "Well, it's not just you. We both end up arguing and
then going off our separate ways. I'd just as soon
avoid that."

You: "I agree. Our discussions haven't ended very well. If
we could come up with a way to prevent us from
arguing or walking off, would you say it would be
worth getting at some of the things that bother
us?"

Dad: "I guess that'd be OK."

And now for your professional conflict:

Boss: "We're so swamped with work right now that I
can't take time to delegate new responsibilities. I
have to make dozens of decisions a day—make that
hundreds. I expect all of you to give me all the
information you have, fast, and then trust me to
deal with things. I like working that way. I'm successful with it."

You: "You're saying that you're really swamped, and that means hundreds of decisions. The way you like to work best is to get our input as fast as possible and then act alone. Is that right?"

Boss: "Exactly."

Try very hard to stay calm, even if your opponent starts to criticize or verbally attack you. *Don't defend yourself immediately (or at all, if possible),* even if you feel hurt and threatened by the person's outburst of feelings and criticism. Allow your opponent to let off steam first. Once the person feels accepted and heard by you, he or she will usually be more ready to reason.

Skill Area: Keeping Track of Your Own Feelings, Needs, and Goals

If you follow our suggestions, you'll know what your feelings, needs, and goals are as you prep for and walk into this meeting. You'll begin the discussion fully aware of what you feel and want to achieve.

We think you should monitor yourself *during* the discussion as well. Particularly when significant issues are being reviewed, you'll be reacting mentally, spiritually, emotionally, and even physically to what's going on. Stay tuned to these important signals, even while you're actively listening. Every few minutes, take a body and feelings check by asking yourself:

- What's my body telling me right now? What does that signal typically mean?
- How am I feeling about what just happened? Am I excited, pleased, and satisfied? Am I having difficulty reading my feelings? Or do I feel slightly afraid or irritated?
- Why am I feeling this?
- How should I express these feelings? Is it appropriate to share them with words or actions right now? Should I try to keep them in check with some prayer? By relaxing my muscles and taking deep breaths to calm me down? Should I call for a break and handle my feelings privately?

Doing this "maintenance check" periodically will help you

recognize what's happening within you and what you need to do next. In chapter 6, we point out some specific ideas you can try if you experience being overwhelmed by feelings—yours or the other party's.

Skill Area: Resolving the Issues, One by One

As we mention above, you and your opponent should have either a mental or a written list of the issues to discuss. We recommend writing down the list, especially when you have quite a few items, and then using the jointly edited list as your first "formal" settlement.

If that seems too formal, make good mental notes, and keep checking with the other person to be sure you both know which issues have been resolved and which haven't.

Each issue on the list must be addressed in detail. Here's one way to tackle the issues on your list.

■ Decide on how to state each issue. Make these statements as objective as you can. Here are some examples:
—"The points to discuss are: how we express affection to each other and what we can do if one of us is irritated with the other. Is that what you see, Dad?"
—"The first issue is the idea of shared decision-making and how I can best help you with the decisions you have to make for our department. The second is yours—the length of my memos—and the third is how I can get feedback on my performance. Do we agree?"

■ Determine the order in which you want to settle each issue. If additional issues come up later, add them to the list and put them in order, too.

■ If you have several issues, say four or more, work on the easiest ones first. If you're not sure which are "easy," test out one or two possibilities. (If you've done your homework, you already know what your opponent wants and where the tough challenges are going to be.)

■ Take turns expressing feelings, concerns, needs, and desired outcomes on the issue being discussed. Allow time for both of you to fully understand the issue as well as the other person's view of it.

■ Propose and discuss two or more alternate solutions for

resolving this first issue. Where appropriate, expand the pie so you can both meet your needs.

- Agree on one of the alternatives and jot it down. Later in the meeting, you'll work out the details on exactly who does what to carry out the agreement.
- Make a positive comment about each issue you resolve and express appreciation to encourage your opponent. For example, "I'm glad we were able to come up with that solution. Thanks for hanging in there!"
- Move on to the next issue.

Experts in negotiation settle issues slowly and systematically. This is one way you can be viewed as a firm negotiator. As a BEST conflict-resolver, you'll combine such strength with gentleness, warmth, flexibility, and generosity so that the negotiation process and outcomes please you, your opponent(s), and God.

We're convinced that by applying negotiation skills in ways that combine seemingly opposite qualities, you'll obey the biblical exhortation to "seek peace, and pursue it" (Ps. 34:14). You'll also perform the role of peacemaker as you "live in peace with one another" (1 Thes. 5:13).

In such a context, power and influence designed to capitalize on your opponents is unacceptable. Rather, teamwork aimed at shared benefits and better ends for you and your opponents are revered.

On the other hand, you may be negotiating with a party who thinks you're naive and wants to take unfair advantage of you. By making concessions slowly and thoughtfully, you communicate your skill and knowledge as an experienced conflict resolver. BEST conflict-resolvers employ skills designed *not* to take advantage of their opponents. BEST skills can be used by you and your adversaries in order to achieve a better end for both sides. Tricks and unfair tactics aimed at taking advantage of someone are inappropriate to the BEST approach. Chapter 9 illustrates some of these.

Skill Area: Quickly Reviewing the Meeting up to Now
Take stock of your performance up to this point. We hope you can say to yourself:

"Nice work up to now! I prepared well for the session and did a good job of scheduling it. I set a positive tone for the discussion and got agreement on the agenda and rules. I'm listening actively and keeping track of my feelings and needs. Thus far, I've tried to hear and appreciate the feelings and needs of the other person."

So far you've resolved one issue in each conflict, and all of you seem satisfied with how you reached your settlements. In the next chapter, you'll continue through the meetings. You'll meet several strong challenges and see some ways of meeting them. You'll also learn how to finalize your agreements and then follow up to be sure the settlements are actually carried out.

Before you go on, try the following experiments. We think they'll help you polish your skills in handling the first part of conflict resolution meetings.

Experiment 9: "What Are the Issues?"

Read the following descriptions of conflicts, and see if you can analyze some of the major issues that are likely to be involved.

A. You (the potential buyer) and a potential seller are about to meet to negotiate the purchase of her home.

   1. Based on your actual personal situation (assume you want to and can afford to buy a house), what do you see as the most important issues to you, in ranked order?
       Issue 1:
       Issue 2:
       Issue 3:
       Issue 4:
       Issue 5:

   2. Why did you position the issues in the order you chose? (Easy ones first? Related issues grouped together?)

B. Your neighbor has announced that he's about to raise chickens. Not only that, but he's planning to sell the eggs out of his front yard. He has joked that he may add some goats and pigs a little later, and he can use your yard for overflow parking. You checked, and there is no town ordinance against his business. You aren't too excited about the plan, so you decide to request a discussion and possible resolution to this conflict.

1. What do you see as three of the main issues in the conflict?

Issue 1:

Issue 2:

Issue 3:

2. Which of your values influenced your selecting each of these three?

C. Your church is considering establishing a child care center for children, infants through six-year-olds, whose parents work. You're chairperson of the committee appointed to study the project. As a good planner, you decide to pinpoint several potentially controversial issues that could come up within the church or within the community to be served by the center.

1. What issues might arise?

Issue 1:

Issue 2:

Issue 3:

Issue 4:

2. How would you specifically word Issue 1 on the printed agenda you'll distribute at the committee meeting tonight?

D. To be certain you're on the right track, discuss your answers with someone you consider a skilled conflict-resolver.

Experiment 10: "A Search for Creative Alternatives"
Read through the following conflict situation, and then complete the activities below.

—*Situation:*You're interested in buying a nice piece of mountain property on which to build a retreat center. Included in the package are 150 acres, a gorgeous river, and the peace and solitude you've been looking for.

Right before you submit your bid on the land, you discover that a gold-mining squatter has been living on part of the land. Using large and noisy equipment, he is busily digging and screening for gold six days a week (twelve hours per day) on the shore of this river.

The courts and the Fish and Game Commission have ruled in favor of the current landowner, but the miner insists he's staying forever. To make things more difficult, the squatter is also a Christian.

A. Brainstorm (with yourself or with someone else) as many alternatives as possible to resolve the above conflict so that both sides gain. Be creative and think of how to "enlarge the pie."

B. List each alternative below.
   1.
   2.
   3.

C. Take a break and think about something else. Then come back and see if some additional creative solutions come to you.
   Additional Idea #1:
   Additional Idea #2:

CHAPTER SIX

Resolving Conflicts, Part II—How to End the Negotiation

We start out OK, but sooner or later one of us says something hurtful and then off we go in another fight. We never get back on track and resolve anything!

—Frustrated negotiator

The end of a matter is better than its beginning.

—Ecclesiastes 7:8

So far, you've learned how to prepare for and begin the so-called "formal conflict resolution meeting." In this chapter, you'll see how to continue the discussion, make appealing proposals to the other party, handle objections, deal with criticism and personal attacks on you, come to closure, and follow up your meeting. We continue to use the hypothetical conflict illustrations you have with your father and your boss.

Skill Area: Taking "Process Checks" along the Way
Skilled negotiators take time in their meetings to see if both sides are comfortable with the way the encounter is going.

We say they're checking the "process" being followed. Instead of barreling along, focusing only on the issues and outcomes and assuming all is well, they pause now and then to see if any changes are needed in procedures.

We recommend that you do these maintenance checks in your discussions. For example, you can ask yourself and the other party, "How are we doing?" or "Do we need to make any adjustments in the way we're proceeding?"

Check your own tension and stress level to see if you're comfortable with the process. Are there any indicators that you're overly nervous or fearful? What's the reason? Are you holding back too much? Sometimes, after systematic practice, you can release part of this excess tension by taking some deep breaths, tensing and then relaxing key muscle areas, and even tell your tight muscles to "relax!"

Another strategy is to comment on what you're experiencing: "To be honest, I'm feeling a little nervous right now. This discussion is really important to me." As a rule of thumb, personal disclosures such as these are most appropriate when your opponent is also a "BEST" negotiator.

When you're dealing with tough opponents, particularly in business settings, you'll generally want to handle your feelings silently (or with other people from your side)—not openly with the other side. They could take unfair advantage of your openness and vulnerability.

If your maintenance check uncovers some dissatisfaction, either of you can *suggest a modification* in the process: "I think it would help if we turned a little more to face each other, turned off the radio, asked each other more questions, went back and restated the issue, and wrote down our concerns as we go."

Your opponent may say, "It's going all right," but act as if he or she is very uncomfortable. You could take the comment at face value and proceed with the agenda. This process of dealing directly with conflicts may be very new to the person, and he or she may get more comfortable as you go on.

On the other hand, you could comment on what you're observing: "Dad, the tone of your voice makes me think you want to tell me something difficult, but you're not sure you should. Is that right?"

These process checks will be very helpful every now and then in your discussion. Questions such as: "How are we doing on time?" "Should we go for another half hour?" or "How about a cup of coffee?" show concern for the comfort of both of you and will help the flow and "climate" of the meeting. They're simple but important techniques in negotiation.

Skill Area: Making Appealing Proposals to the Other Side

Effective negotiation is much more than listening to the other side's needs and making sure the process is going smoothly. You must also be able to present your needs and desired outcomes *in a way that will appeal to the other party.* How can you do this?

Here are some suggestions that have worked for us and others we've observed:

- Present the idea so that the other party can see the *benefit to him or her,* not only the benefit to you. ("If you approve my taking this seminar, you'll be able to assign the bookkeeping to me and free up several hours for yourself every week.")
- If the other side tends to appreciate logic and objectivity, use *strong facts and reasons* to support your idea. ("This will work for three reasons. One, the machine is guaranteed for a year. Two, the leads already know how to use it. Three...")
- If your opponent isn't excited about facts and reasons but responds to feelings, build enthusiasm by *showing your own excitement and describing your "dream"* as you see it. ("I can hardly sit still as I think about it! I can see the two of us sitting on the boat, cruising down the Delta, feeling the sun on our faces, laughing like a couple of kids, pulling in the fish for dinner.")
- *Use the other person's actual words and build on his or her ideas.* Your opponent will recognize and respond to ideas and proposals that are familiar.

- *Say only as much as needed* to get the other person to agree. Once you're successful, stop. Don't go on and on, adding additional points or the person may have second thoughts. ("Why is she selling so hard?")
- Make it *easy for the person to say "yes."* Think through the details and opposing arguments in advance. Have routine forms typed and ready to sign. Offer to do the legwork (or phone calls, or difficult confrontations with others) for the person.
- *Ask directly what it would take* to make the other person agree. ("Exactly what would it take for you to accept my proposal?")
- *Offer "rewards"* for doing what you ask. ("If you agree, I'll write a letter to your boss outlining the excellent service you've given us.")

Do you feel uneasy about the rewards idea? To many people, this sounds like a bribe or buying the person's favor. In our opinion, rewards are ethical and acceptable provided you: (1) tell the person in advance what you're offering, (2) give the choice to participate or not, and (3) make it totally acceptable to refuse the offer.

What isn't acceptable is to manipulate by secretly rewarding the individual for doing what you want. Furthermore, coercing participation because of your power ("I'm your husband, that's why!") or in some way giving punishment later for refusals is improper behavior. As we assert in chapter 5, BEST conflict-resolvers use nonmanipulative skills and strive for considerateness as well as firmness.

The important things to keep in mind as you present your ideas are the needs and style of your opponent. Tailor your presentation to appeal to this person.

Skill Area: Handling Objections to Your Ideas

Let's say you've presented a brilliant, well-conceived idea, one that utilized several of the suggestions listed above. But your opponent is resisting. His or her answer is "no." What do you do then?

Probe for underlying reasons. Take a moment to decide what no really means in this situation. The person may mean absolutely no, not now, and not later. On the other hand, it's very possible that no means: (1) not now; (2) not important as far as I can see; (3) not able; (4) not enough information; or (5) not in that form.

No could mean "maybe" or even "yes, if..." We suggest you probe a little further and *try to uncover the reasons behind the objection*. Let's go back to your discussion with your father.

> You: "I want to understand your reasons for not wanting to express affection the ways I suggested. What is it that bothers you about the idea?"

> Dad: "It's just not necessary. We can show our feelings in other ways besides all that touchy, feely stuff. My family never did that. It's better to do things for one another, help them with the chores, for example. Besides, we're too old for that."

What's your dad really saying? What are his real reasons for saying no to words of affection and accompanying hugs and kisses? Without knowing more of the background, we can only guess the following.

Chances are he believes sweet words and physical demonstration of affection are unnecessary and even wrong, selfish, or examples of poor parenting. It may be very difficult to help him change his thinking on such long-standing beliefs. On the other hand, he may be saying, "I'm not able" because he lacks the skills and experience to make these gestures. He may think he'll look silly or be rebuffed by you if he does it "wrong." He may be fearful of any touching because of what he's heard about child abuse.

You might check out some possibilities with him. Begin with an affirming statement and then summarize what you think you've heard.

> You: "Your objections are very understandable to me. *(Notice, while affirming him, you didn't say "acceptable to me.")* Let me be sure I have it right. You're against the idea because to you these gestures aren't necessary—maybe even selfish and wrong for parents and kids to do. And this is a long shot—maybe you don't want to because you haven't

done it much and think maybe I wouldn't like the way you did it. Is that possible?"

If you're nondefensive and have proved yourself trustable so far in the negotiation, the other party may tell you the real reasons, or at least part of them. This is where hidden issues start to surface. So be sensitive and probe for them.

Once you uncover your opponent's reasons, your next move is to supply what's needed: additional information (such as specifics on what you're proposing); examples of how it has worked elsewhere (with the two of you or with others); offer to help with implementation; or possibly a dose of reassurance.

. Remember that your opponent will usually need some additional time:

■ to trust you;
■ to understand and get used to your ideas;
■ to evaluate and see the possible worth of your proposals;
■ to modify his or her own ideas.

If you can, suggest a temporary trial test of your idea to see if it can work. Here are some other alternatives to try when you meet objections.

The Broken Record. This is a strategy to use only in certain situations. The technique is helpful when the other person is being unreasonably stubborn, making weak excuses, or denying responsibility for his or her part in the situation.

The "broken record" technique requires you to gently but firmly insist on what you want. If the person refuses, you state your request again, like the sound of a skip on a scratched record. Each time the person refuses, you once again calmly, but firmly state your request. You can vary your language or keep it the same each time. Both of us have used this successfully on the telephone when we've met with what seemed like unreasonable resistance.

You: "I would like your firm to send me a letter of apology and to refund my payment in full."

Owner: "I'm sorry, our company policy doesn't allow us to do that."

You: "I would like your firm to send me a letter of

> apology within the next four days and to refund
> my payment in full."
>
> Owner: "I really can't do that."
>
> You: "I want your firm to send me a letter of apology
> within the next four days and to refund my pay-
> ment in full."
>
> Owner: "Oh, all right. What's your address?"

Avoid Blaming Language. If the other party continues to resist or tries to put you down for your suggestions, you'll probably be tempted to lash out and blame your adversary for ruining the negotiations. Do whatever it takes to resist using any of the following language:

- "Why can't you ever _____ (listen to me, think of someone besides yourself, be a good father)?"
- "Don't you even care that _____ (I'm hurting inside, I'm trying to solve this, we have a problem here)?"
- "If you really loved me, you'd _____ (do what I'm asking, stop being so stubborn, be kind for a change)."

By making remarks such as these, you'll only put the other person on the defensive and turn the discussion into an argument.

Instead, maintain composure and return to resolving the issue. Take some deep breaths, bite your cheek, dig your nails into your palm, and, if necessary, call for a time-out to let off steam and refocus your approach.

Avoid Bringing Up Old Issues. If you're particularly frustrated at this point, you may be tempted to bring up unresolved issues from the past. Or you may bring up a new issue that suddenly occurs to you.

Resist these urges because they're surefire ways to bog down and even destroy your resolution meeting. Stick to the issue at hand and either resolve it or, by mutual agreement, postpone it until you've resolved the current issue on the agenda. Insist that your opponent follows the same rule.

Skill Area: Handling Personal Attacks on You

From time to time, you'll be faced with someone who criticizes or even attacks you verbally. Believe it or not, these unpleasant moments can actually be blessings in disguise. We want to offer some suggestions for handling them and for turning them into opportunities. These attacks can be sources of information as well as times for you to demonstrate strength plus caring.

Let's use your conflict with your boss to demonstrate several things you can do. Assume that the two of you have been having a good discussion for, the past thirty minutes. You've successfully resolved the issue about your memo-writing (they'll be shorter and submitted by 10 A.M. daily).

Now you're on the touchier issue of her decision-making. After exchanging some feelings about decision-making in general (it's exciting and somewhat unsettling for both of you), you do a good job of checking out her preferences for how the two of you should proceed.

Things seem to be going well when all of a sudden the look on her face changes, and she practically shouts at you: "You're so pushy and demanding! You want everything your way, don't you? Including your career handed to you on a silver platter!"

You're caught by surprise, so your first reaction is to resort to one of the extreme styles we outline in chapter 3. If you're basically a conflict *avoider*, you'll want to pretend you didn't hear it, change the subject, or suggest you end the meeting and get some rest.

If you're an *accommodator*, you'll be inclined to apologize for anything you might have said or done to upset her. Then you'll give in on the issue. Your goal is to preserve the peace and your relationship at all costs.

If you're a *competer*, your impulse will be to attack back, criticizing her in even stronger terms.

We recommend that you don't resort to any of these extremes. Instead, try one or more of the following ideas for dealing with personal attacks. They deal with the issue, show respect for the person, and aim for the ultimate goal—a better end for both of you.

First of all, *paraphrase what you think you've heard* (to buy a little time and to prevent any misunderstanding on your part). By all means, avoid any blaming language and

avoid bringing up old issues. You don't want an argument!
Here are some more BEST ideas you can try:

- *Thank the person* for the information. ("Thanks for explaining your viewpoint so clearly and forcefully.")
- Surprise your opponent by *agreeing with any truth* in the statement. ("You're right, I can be pushy and demanding at times.") This technique is called "fogging." A fogbank doesn't hit back; it simply absorbs the blow. Don't agree with all of the statement—only with what you agree is true.
- Narrow down the generalization by *asking the person to be specific.* ("What specifically don't you like about how I request or push for things?" This technique is called "sectioning." Often it will reveal only a small point, but one that's irritating or concerning your opponent.
- Try to *turn the attack on you into an attack on the problem.* ("You have every right to expect me to be fair in how I act with you. What we need is a way I can get my requests known where you will not feel pushed.")

This last technique is called "reframing." To do it correctly, you must focus on your opponent's "good intent." (Yes, you should believe he or she has one!) This creates the image of you and your opponent as a team on one side of the table, while the problem or mutual goal is on the other. Here are some more examples of reframing:

Attack	*Reframed Response*
"You're the laziest housekeeper I've ever seen!"	"You're right in insisting on good cleaning standards for our house. What we need is a strategy that will help us meet those standards."
"You never visit your mother and me. You're so selfish and mean to us."	"I agree that I'm not showing you and Mom enough that I care. Let's find a way that I can show you I do and yet still take care of my marriage, the kids, and my job."

Reframing takes practice! We're still working on doing it better, so don't be discouraged if the skill comes slowly.

Skill Area: Continuing through the Rest of Your Issues

Now you know more about how to explore feelings and issues, present proposals for resolutions, handle objections, and deal with personal attacks. Continue to use these skills as you work through the other issues on your agenda.

Be sure to do regular process checks as you move along. Stay aware of your feelings and tension level. Also, we suggest that you keep notes of decisions and any unfinished business as you go. This will make your next step, getting closure, go more smoothly and quickly.

Skill Area: Getting Closure

Many beginning negotiators omit this important part of the resolution process. Excited that their opponents seem to agree on the issue(s), they end the meeting abruptly, thank God for getting them through it, and start celebrating!

Unfortunately, when this happens both parties often walk away with completely different understandings about what was decided. Just as bad, the agreements are never implemented. Each side thinks the other party will forget those resolutions in time, or the other party will do all the work.

Don't make these strategic mistakes. Before you go out the door, *write down exactly what the two sides have agreed.* At the very least, make notes and agree that one of you will write up the settlement and get it to the other party for approval within, for example, a week.

We suggest that, for each issue, you get an agreement on at least the following points:

- Name of the issue
- Agreed on settlement of the issue
- Who is responsible for doing what to implement the settlement
- Dates by which the implementation tasks are to be started and/or completed
- How you'll monitor or check on the implementation

- Any rewards for completing the tasks
- Any penalties for not completing the tasks
- Date for reviewing the agreement

Here's how this might look for one of the conflict issues with your boss. Let's say you write the agreement in the form of a draft memo which you send to her for her polishing and final agreement.

SAMPLE DRAFT MEMORANDUM

TO: Maggie
FROM: Kim
DATE:
SUBJECT: Our Settlements Regarding Decisions, Memos, and Feedback to Me
Issue: *How you will include me in future departmental decision-making.*

Our settlements:

- For a trial period of one month:
  —we will collaborate on at least three major departmental decisions;
  —You agree to tell me as early as possible about upcoming decisions, brief me on their context, and ask me for input orally or in writing.
  —I agree to present to you short, to-the-point suggestions with backup rationale and data as needed.
  —You will provide feedback on the quality of my input plus suggestions for improvement.
- We will begin implementing these on _____.
- We agree to meet and review progress on these agreements the week of _____.
- If we follow through on our commitments, we agree to have a terrific lunch at your expense, of course!

Skill Area: Ending Your Meeting on a Positve Note
Consider one last thing before you end your negotiation meeting. *End on a positive note that sets the tone for future encounters.* Express your appreciation to the other side for agreeing to meet and for working through the issues. Stress the shared gains that you both achieved.

If appropriate, pray together thanking God for His help throughout the process and seek guidance and energy to implement your settlements.

Finally, use an appropriate form of touch to cement your good feelings. Shake hands, squeeze the person's shoulder, or even offer a hug that says, "This was hard work and worth it! I'm looking forward to talking with you again next time."

Skill Area: Following Up Later

After the meeting, you still have work to do. To be certain the agreements are carried out, finalize the written agreement and be sure that both sides have copies. Follow through on the tasks you've agreed to.

Take time by yourself to evaluate the session. What went the way you had hoped? What would you do differently next time? If appropriate, meet or talk on the phone with the other party to debrief your meeting and discuss how you both felt about it. Consider dropping this person a note to express your appreciation for participating in the process of resolution.

To be sure your settlements are carried out to a continued better end, monitor each other (in the way you both agreed). Catch any deviations before they become large and threaten to destroy your settlement.

Don't give up if you didn't resolve all issues on the agenda. Remember the importance of tenacity, hanging in there until the issues are resolved to your satisfaction. Work on setting up another meeting. Go back to the beginning on the remaining issues and be sure you do your homework on each one. Chapter 8 presents further strategies to consider, including using a mediator, if the issues are too difficult for the two of you to resolve.

This is how the Better End Strategy works with personal and professional conflicts. Now that you've seen how to use the BEST with individuals, it's time to increase your ability to settle conflicts within and between organizations. Before you go on to this challenge, however, polish your new skills in the experiments below.

Experiment 11: "Handling Objections and Attacks"
This experiment is designed to sharpen your skills in handling your opponents' objections to your proposals as well as verbal attacks directed at you.
A. Read each "opponent's comment" listed below. Under each one, write a possible BEST response you could make.
   1. "I don't think that solution is going to work."

   2. "That meal you cooked wasn't very good."

   3. "You give lousy presentations."

   4. "You're so self-righteous. I'm sick of your holier-than-thou attitude!"

   5. "You're a terrible mother (father). When I'm eighteen, I'm leaving!"

   6. "You don't know what you're talking about."

   7. "Well, I guess we could try that idea, but..."

   8. "You're just like your father!"

   9. "Can't you ever do anything right?"

   10. "I really don't know how to hug you."

B. Consider discussing your responses with someone else who is working on conflict resolution skills.

Experiment 12: "Plan for an Upcoming Meeting"
Think of a real interpersonal conflict you're in, one in which it would make sense to set up a resolution meeting.
A. Fill out this tentative plan to prepare for the session.

MY TENTATIVE MEETING PLAN:

1. Person with whom I have this conflict:

2. Information on myself:
   - What I see as the causes of the conflict:

   - Key issue(s) to be resolved:

   - My feelings about the person and the issue(s):

   - Alternatives I see for resolving the conflict:

   - My Best Alternative to a Negotiated Agreement (BATNA):

3. Information on the other party:
   - Probable feelings toward me and the issue(s):

   - Probable goals or desired outcomes of this negotiation:

   - Probable BATNA:

   - Typical style or approach in handling conflicts such as this one:

4. Possible times and places we might be able to meet:
   - Times:
   - Locations:

5. What I could say in my invitation:

6. How I'd like to extend the invitation (by phone, in person, in writing) and why:

B. If appropriate, show this tentative plan to someone you trust. Ask for feedback on what you've prepared.

CHAPTER SEVEN

Dealing with Organizational Conflict

And we urge you, brethren, admonish the unruly, encourage the fainthearted, help the weak, be patient with all men. See that no one repays another with evil for evil, but always seek after that which is good for one another and for all men.

—1 Thessalonians 5:14-15

The Apostle Paul gave this sound counsel to the members of an organization in conflict, the community of early Christians who lived, worked, worshiped, and had disagreements in Thessalonica. Since you are a member of numerous organizations in conflict, we want to use this chapter to build on Paul's wisdom and show how you can apply what you've learned already to the organizations with which you're involved.

In the preceding chapters, you learned strategies for resolving personal and professional conflicts in any area of your life. Most of the illustrations provided were one-to-one situations.

But what happens when you find yourself in the middle of a group of people in conflict? What do you do when your organization is having a dispute—internally or with some outside group? Before we offer some suggestions, let's take a closer look at organizations in general.

What's an Organization?

An organization is *any group(s) of people who interact with each other in order to pursue common goals.* Notice the key words: "group," "interact," and "common goals." Using this definition, a family is an organization. So is a film production company, a church, or a basketball team. Most of us are involved with a number of organizations at any one time. It's a fact that organizations and potential organizational conflicts abound!

In our seminars we like to promote the concept of "healthy," as opposed to "unhealthy," organizations. The vital, alive groups have a number of conflict-related characteristics which help them remain strong. Here are a few of the key ones:

- Their separate internal "systems" depend on each other. There is a constant give-and-take negotiation across "division" lines. (For example, in such a setting the Engineering division of a firm needs and values the Sales department and vice versa.)
- They strike a happy balance between meeting the needs of the organization and those of their members. If a business doesn't reach its profit goal, employee expectations of promotions and raises are seldom met. On the other hand, if employees aren't rewarded, they'll resist helping the organization succeed.
- They keep growing and adapting like healthy plants, animals, and humans. A large part of growing and adapting comes from successful conflict resolution.

Our ideas on handling organizational conflict tie into these features of healthy organizations. Specifically, the Better End Strategy addresses the following:

- *Interdependence among systems and groups*—Seldom does one side have all the necessary information to solve problems and create innovative solutions. Using the BEST, opposing sides must probe for and share information with each other, then seek creative alternatives that allow both sides to gain.

The Sale and Engineering departments (in conflict over meeting customers' requests) share information on the product. The Sales force tells the engineers what the customers don't like and listens carefully to Engineering's design problems. Engineering, in turn, listens to Sales' practical feedback and also suggests ideas that Sales can teach the customers about using the product. Both sides get closer to their goals.

- *Balance between individual and organizational needs*—The BEST encourages open and honest communication rather than hidden agendas. Trust is consciously built, information is continually shared, and both sides participate in decisions. Numerous companies now allow their employees to participate in organizational planning and profit sharing. Even if they don't use the term, a version of the BEST helps them to resolve conflicts.

- *Growth and adaptation*—Finally, since healthy organizations need to grow and adapt in order to survive, they need positive ways to handle the inevitable conflicts that arise. Unfair, unprincipled attempts at resolving issues will eventually hurt and even destroy organizations. We've seen examples of businesses, churches, and other organizations that eventually failed because they didn't use healthy ways of resolving conflicts. We think the fair and principled approach of the Better End Strategy can help all organizations become healthier.

Building On Your One-to-One Conflict Resolution Skills

You'll be glad to know that your one-on-one skills will also work in organizations. To better manage conflicts in these settings, you can adopt and adapt the skills you acquired in earlier chapters. Keep in mind, however, that planning and implementation is even more difficult in organizations.

For example, as you try to determine the other party's

needs and desired outcomes in advance of any negotiation session, remember that now you face multiple parties! That means you're up against multiple points of view, negotiation histories, needs for recognition, and conflict resolution skills! Needs and desired outcomes won't be as obvious as cautious individuals try to wait out and second-guess each other. Your most appropriate strategies are to move slowly and carefully build people's trust in you.

In a group setting the strategies you try to implement will require much more time. More decision-makers will have to review and give their opinions on every issue. People will be anxious to preserve the status quo because their ways took a long time to get established in the organization. You should keep reminding yourself that healthy organizations must change and adapt. Make sure you allow plenty of time for improvements to occur. You will need to spend considerable time "selling" your ideas and showing how they'll help both individuals and the organization.

You'll also be faced with many meetings. Many of these will seem like a waste of time, but organizations are committed to them. Some even thrive on them. The best advice is to accept these many meetings as inevitable and to streamline the meetings for which you're responsible.

Following up any agreements made in an organizational conflict will be even more challenging than it was in your one-to-one conflicts. You must keep in mind that interdependent systems in an organization are complicated. Be the "squeaky wheel." Cheerfully and optimistically go back to people again and again. Remember to give credit and thanks to everyone who helps move the process along.

Particularly in unhealthy organizations, you may face a lot of survival *game-playing and unprincipled negotiation tactics*. Accept this fact as a way of life in many organizations, but hold onto your own principled negotiation approach. Study chapter nine's discussion on unfair tactics so you won't be naive and unprepared. Allow your ethical stance to serve as an example and witness as well as a technique for others to imitate.

If you use your repertoire of individual skills, you'll do

well in most organizational conflicts. There is much more to learn, however, so let's turn now to some new skills that are useful in group settings.

Tackling Group Conflict

First, we offer a caveat. To become an expert at organizational conflict resolution and the specialty of "organization development," you'll need much more training than we can give in this book. Library sections, college degrees, and entire professions are dedicated to these difficult areas of expertise. Those who excel in these venues are good at a number of skills, among them:

- analyzing organizational behavior;
- building productive, satisfied teams;
- diagnosing problems in organizations;
- mediating among dissenting groups;
- using many types of strategic interventions to remedy organizational problems.

Since this is an introductory book on conflict resolution, we can't go into all of these areas. What we offer here, however, are three skills to help you take initial steps toward resolving organizational conflicts. These skills include the following:

1. Knowing when and how to use a conflict resolution "team."
2. Conducting an organizational conflict resolution session.
3. Using the "single text procedure" as one of your BEST tools.

Organizational Skill 1: Knowing When and How to Use a Conflict Resolution "Team"

Sometimes, instead of working by yourself, it makes sense to use a "team" of people to resolve an organizational conflict. On the other hand, a team isn't always the best answer.

One church we know was struggling over its senior minister, who had held his position for over a decade. Increasingly, he was becoming more authoritarian in his administration and management of the organization. It was becoming "his church" with his having the final say on most issues.

Opposition by staff members was discouraged; dissenters were encouraged to find jobs elsewhere.

Several staff vented their frustration to each other, but no one was willing to talk to the minister about it. Finally, one staff member went to friends in the congregation, told them about the minister's actions, and took a delegation of five people to confront the minister about his behavior.

Was this a good team approach? We don't think so, as much as we like and encourage teamwork in many situations. In this case, the "team" was premature and made up of the wrong people.

Let's take a look at what Jesus said about confrontation: "If your brother sins against you, go to him privately and confront him with his fault. If he listens and confesses it, you have won back a brother. But if not, then take one or two others with you and go back to him again, proving everything you say by these witnesses" (Matt. 18:15-16, TLB).

Applying this to the church conflict, the staff member is to meet with the minister *in private* to confront him. If he doesn't admit his error and change, the staffer is to take another along and try again, still quietly and in private.

Jesus goes on to say that if the accused still doesn't make a change the challengers can "go public," that is, bring the matter up with the church. We believe that first means the church's governing board or elders. At that time, a team could be pulled together to investigate and resolve the issues.

Linda remembers one time she blew this initial skill in an organizational conflict. She was one of the supervisors in a language school in what was then Saigon, South Vietnam. Her teachers and students finished morning classes several minutes later than another supervisor's teachers and students. When the other department finished, everyone rushed down the stairs for lunch, making a lot of noise and disrupting Linda's classes.

After stewing about the conflict for too long, Linda wrongly tried to rally a "team" to her side. She complained to her teachers, angrily stomped downstairs, and reported her frustration to the school principal. He promptly called the other supervisor, teachers, and students on the carpet. The result? The other supervisor was furious at Linda for not bringing up the issue with him (he wasn't even aware of the disruption until then) and for embarrassing him and his department in front of the principal. It took months to heal the relationship and to get the two departments back into a healthy interdependence.

Had Linda privately approached the other supervisor, the issue would probably have been resolved quickly and to everyone's satisfaction.

When does the team approach make sense? Here are a few rules of thumb to help you decide. Use a team of two (up to a maximum of six) people when:

- you reach an impasse or deadlock in your individual efforts to get the other party to change;
- both sides are willing to have a team investigate and try to resolve the conflict;
- more than you and the other party will be involved in carrying out the settlement. (In this case, be sure the team represents all different views.)

Here's an example of a situation in which a team approach worked very well. Two small businesses that we'll call Company A and Company B were considering a merger. They manufactured similar products and competed for the same market. A merger looked feasible, but the two groups had a major conflict over personnel policies.

Because of this, the employees of Company B, which had flexible work scheduling to meet employee preferences, reacted negatively from the onset of the merger talks. Company A's employees, used to tight structure and teamwork, were fearful of the "flakes" in the other organization.

Instead of moving ahead with the merger and trying to force adoption of either or both systems, the two owners decided to pull together a team of employees from both organizations to resolve the conflict and present a proposal to the management team. The result: the merger went through and the resulting personnel policies for the new organization were better than the two original systems.

We have a few suggestions for you to consider as you participate in a conflict resolution team:

■ Allow time for team members to get acquainted and feel comfortable working together.

■ As early as possible, decide what the group's goals and tasks are—which "better ends" group members want to reach.

■ Choose a team leader who wants the job, has skill in facilitating group discussion, and can inspire others to do their tasks.

■ Strike a balance between the needs of individuals and the overall needs of the organizations.

■ Get something accomplished early so the team feels good about itself and its work.

The task of resolving an important organizational conflict is a difficult one, but it can be one of the most significant accomplishments any group can make. In the next skill area, you'll learn some details of how to design and put on an organizational conflict resolution meeting.

Organizational Skill 2: Conducting a Large-Group Conflict Resolution Session

We've offered a number of suggestions in this book about conflict resolution meetings, but in this skill area we address one way you can design and conduct a particular kind of negotiation meeting. It combines some techniques of a process called "team-building" as well as group conflict resolution.

Let's assume your small conflict resolution team has met as a group, participated in several lively yet productive meetings, and identified some tentative issues. It came to an important decision—that all members of both opposing groups should get together face-to-face to resolve those issues.

You propose the idea to the leader of your organization, and the idea is accepted. Not only is this a good idea, but there's money in the budget to meet off-site for the day— with lunch thrown in! You're pleased with the news, but wary of the responsibility. What do you do now?

One approach that has worked well for us and for other organizational consultants is found in Figure 1. Feel free to adapt the ideas for your own organization.

SUGGESTIONS FOR A LARGE-GROUP SESSION

1. Reserve a quiet place to hold the session. The location doesn't have to be luxurious, but it should be away from telephones and other interruptions. Provide some separate rooms for small-group discussions. Tell everyone to come in casual clothes and bring along snacks and drinks. The mood should be informal.

2. Before the session, interview a representative sample of the entire group to be sure you and the rest of the planning team are aware of any hidden issues. Assure people you won't mention specific names, but will anonymously share the information they provide with the rest of the group. (Make a point of disguising any obvious information sources.)

3. With your teammates, analyze the interview data before the session. Figure out any trends you see. What's mentioned by two or more people? List these issues in short phrases on large, visible pieces of paper that can be posted in front of the big group at the session.

4. Kick off the resolution session with food and a positive statement by one of your organization's leaders. ("I know we can all agree that we're here today to discuss conflicts, listen to each other's views and ideas, and come up with strategies that will make our lives easier.")

5. Have the team lead the group in an exercise that begins to uncover the groups needs and issues. One we like is used by a conflict-resolver we admire, Warren Schmidt, of the University of Southern California. It goes like this:

■   Ask each opposing side (management vs. employees, Department A vs. Department B) to go off by itself and complete the following:
    —"We really like it when you _____ " (This "trigger phrase" forces positive recognition of the other

side's good efforts as well as prompting this side to identify its needs and desired outcomes.)

—"Our lives would be easier if you would _____." (A phrase to pull out additional needs and desired outcomes.)

—"We think your lives would be easier if we would _____." (This forces recognition of the other side's needs.)

- Have recorders for each side note the answers on separate large pieces of paper to be posted later.
- Bring the sides back together and take turns asking each side to share its findings. (The "listening" side can only ask questions to clarify; it cannot defend itself.)
- When the lists of findings are posted, let people walk around and review them before sitting down again.
- Ask for comments and any generalizations that people notice. Have a recorder who prints well note these on large paper in front of the group.

6. After a break, reassemble and have the planning team present its summary of issues uncovered during its earlier interviews. Rather than repeat points made in the earlier exercise, mention only new information. Invite comments from the group.

7. Once the master list of issues has been presented, have the group prioritize items by a show of hands.

8. Choose the top three issues and divide the large group into smaller work units to determine action steps for resolving these conflicts as quickly as possible. Be sure recorders take notes of all suggestions made.

9. Reassemble the large group again and get reports from the small groups.

10. If time permits, develop some of the specifics of a resolution plan for one of the key issues. Assign individuals or teams to work on specific implementation plans for the remaining conflicts. These should be completed and circulated within the next few days or weeks. (This relates to the "single-text procedure" we outline in the third skill area below.)

11. It is crucial to end the session with a summary of

accomplishments and congratulations to all participants. Reiterate the date the resolution plans are due.

The proposed outline details one version of a group conflict resolution session. If you uncover the issues and come
up with ideas for resolving at least one of them, your meeting should be a success. For many people there, this will be
the first time they've ever worked in such a productive
atmosphere.

Keep two cautions in mind related to this second skill.
First, not every organizational conflict requires this type of
large-group process. Most issues can and must, in the interest of time, be resolved one-to-one or in small groups.

Second, don't schedule large group meetings which start
and end as complaint sessions. Participants will resent having their views aired and hopes raised with no resulting
action. If you're not sure whether it makes sense to have a
large-group conflict resolution session, get some expert
advice.

Organizational Skill 3: Using the One-Text Procedure

Fisher and Ury mention the one-text procedure as a useful
tool for getting settlements in groups of people. It's a technique we use a great deal, so we expand on their description here.

The procedure can work one of two ways. In both, you as
one of the group members, volunteer to be the note taker.
Brian enters most conflict resolution sessions with notepad
and pen in hand and makes this remark: "I volunteer to be
secretary unless someone else wants to take notes." He's
seldom usurped in this role since most people hate to take
minutes. They fail to recognize the tremendous power of
the "secretary."

In the first version of the procedure, as issues are resolved and settled, the note taker writes down each resolution. He or she gets the group to agree on the exact wording, reading it back until everyone is satisfied. Before the
meeting is adjourned, this person summarizes the agreements and volunteers to send everyone a copy afterward.

A second version of the procedure is used when the two sides have difficulty agreeing. Instead of wasting time and antagonizing both parties, the recorder volunteers to write up a tentative resolution based on everyone's input in the discussion. This "single text" is then passed back and forth between the opposing sides at strategic intervals in the meeting or after the meeting adjourns. Usually we find that people accept what they see written on the paper. If they make changes, the corrections are generally minor ones. They've had a chance to work through their feelings and view the exchange from a distance. The printed text by its nature adds to that objectivity.

We've seen cases in which two parties that could barely sit together in the same room come to very principled and caring resolutions using the one-text procedure.

If you use this tool, try the following:

■ Take accurate and thorough notes.

■ Feel free to telephone the parties after the meeting and before you write the summary in order to correct any of your misperceptions, fill in gaps, and shape the accuracy of your records.

■ Include your own suggestions for resolutions if the parties didn't provide them.

■ Circulate the text within a week or ten days of the meeting.

■ Let the parties know how to make changes; include a deadline. ("If I don't hear from you by _____, I'll assume you agree.")

The staff in conflict with the senior minister used a variation of the single-text procedure. The elders called in an outside facilitator to work with the entire staff, including the minister.

The issue of the minister's management style proved a sensitive one, and it would have been difficult for this particular group to discuss changes face-to-face. Consequently, the facilitator worked closely with the minister to coach him on his style and to draft a proposed new set of administrative guidelines. This text was exchanged back and forth with staff members and elders until all were satisfied.

Yes, the one-text is a simple tool. However, it's one that's not used enough in resolving organizational conflicts.

We have another observation for you to consider as you move toward handling organizational conflicts more effectively: You may not be the best person to resolve the conflict at hand. For example, you may be: (1) too new to appreciate the history and difficulty of the conflict; (2) too close to the issues or the people and unable to see objective solutions; or (3) lacking adequate skills or experience in any of the areas we've outlined.

If any of these are true, we encourage you to take the problem to someone who can help. Chapter 8 presents some alternatives, including using a mediator or arbitrator. One of these experts may be the best strategy.

Before you go on, complete the two practical experiments below. They'll sharpen your skills for handling organization conflict.

Experiment 13: "My Private Life as an OCR"

Assume you want to be a better Organizational Conflict-Resolver (OCR). One approach is to analyze how well you've performed up to now, build on your successes and strengths, as well as identify and work on areas where you need to improve.

A. Select an incident during which you became immersed in a conflict in an organization or between organizations. It could be one you currently face. Assess your performance while answering the following questions.

1. What was one of the basic issues?

2. What are two or three things you did that were effective (before, during, or after the negotiation session)?

3. How did you know those actions were effective?

4. Which of your actions would you use again in another organizational conflict?

5. Which actions would you like to improve before you become immersed in another conflict?

6. What skills will you need to acquire in order to make the improvements you desire?

7. How will you go about learning those skills?

B. Discuss what you've written with someone skilled in handling organizational conflict.

Experiment 14: "Where Can We Agree Regarding This Organizational Conflict?"

When opposing sides can find initial areas of agreement, they can usually move further toward settling their differences. This exercise will help you assist others to recognize their mutual needs, accomplishments, and goals.

A. For each of the following five conflicts, write at least two features on which each side might agree before it tackles the issues in dispute. Develop answers that will encourage the opponents and strengthen their bond for working cooperatively on conflict resolution. Avoid answers which are defeating statements, such as: "We agree we sure have a problem!" or "We all know this negotiation is going to drag out."

1. Two church factions disputing a doctrinal issue:
   a.
   b.

2. Two community nonprofit agencies competing for limited United Way funding.
   a.
   b.

3. A company's sales team at odds with production staff over apparent difficulties shipping products on schedule to customers.
   a.
   b.

4. A farm workers' union intensely displeased with grape growers who insist on using pesticides on their crops.
   a.
   b.

5. Two countries holding diametrically opposed interpretations of America's Cup rules for sailing competitions.
   a.
   b.

B. Review your statements with someone experienced as an OCR. Congratulate yourself on answers you both agree are creative and constructive for building cooperation. For the others, agree on ways you could strengthen them.

CHAPTER EIGHT

When Nothing Seems to Work

If possible, so far as it depends on you, be at peace with all men.

—*Romans 12:18*

To sum up, let all be harmonious, sympathetic, brotherly, kindhearted, and humble in spirit, not returning evil for evil, or insult for insult, but giving a blessing instead; for you were called for the very purpose that you might inherit a blessing.

—*1 Peter 3:8-9*

How ideal it sounds—living at peace, in harmony, with everyone! We're thankful for the two caveats the Apostle Paul couples with his advice to the Romans: "If possible" and "so far as it depends on you."

Sometimes, even though you negotiate your side of an issue in an excellent, honorable, and shared benefits manner, you run into a dead end. Be prepared for it. Even if you follow every guideline we suggest in this book, you can still reach the point when you and the other side are stuck short of final settlement.

At that time, most of us are tempted to give up in despair.

And the obstacle isn't always a dead end over a monumental issue, such as whether Christian principles will be honored.

In reviewing why negotiations go wrong, Bazerman (1986) concludes that:

> The competitive context of the negotiation adds to the likelihood of escalation. Unilaterally giving up or even reducing demands seems like defeat, while escalating commitment leaves the future uncertain. It is easy for negotiators to see this uncertain future as more desirable than the certain loss of concession (p. 57).

Many of us hate to come in second. That possibility can produce a wall and make the Better End Strategy go awry.

"Impasse" vs. "Deadlock"

An "impasse" in a conflict resolution process is the point where you and your opponent can't agree on a solution that's acceptable to both of you. You're stuck, and no one wants to move, at least for the moment.

In conflict resolution jargon, an impasse is not the same as a "deadlock" ("standoff"). An impasse is more temporary, and particularly with experienced negotiators, optimism regarding settlement still runs high. Deadlocks, at least on the surface, appear permanent.

We suggest that you consider any stall in your negotiations to¹ be an impasse rather than a permanent deadlock.

If you and your opponent seem to be stalled, with no resolution in sight, here are some ideas to try in order to get through the impasse. This time, we'll use a child custody and visitation conflict as our example:

■ Summarize the dilemma. ("It's obvious that we can't agree at this point. You feel very strongly that you should have Timmy with you every weekend and one weekday night. You also want him for the whole summer. I feel just as strongly that he should be with me on school nights and with you every other weekend. I think summers should be negotiated, depending on

Timmy's needs and activities. Is that how you see the disagreement?)

■ Reframe the dilemma as a search for a new and better solution. ("What we need is a way to give Timmy the right amount and kind of time he needs with each of us.") This may inspire a renewed search for a creative solution.

■ Probe for hidden needs and issues. ("I sense you're very concerned that Timmy is pulling away from you and are afraid it will get worse after the divorce. Is that true?") Doing this will often uncover other previously hidden needs and lead to solutions that meet all of the issues.

■ Submit (or concede) with pleasure. ("You're an excellent parent, and I want to make this as smooth as possible for Timmy. I'll agree to your proposal.")

■ Agree in part. ("I can agree to your weeknight request, especially if you can coach him on his math.") This strategy is actually a compromise. You give up part of what you originally wanted. The other person is also expected to give up part of his or her original request.

■ Agree on a trial basis. ("I'm willing to try one weeknight for the next month and see how it goes. If it's a strain for any of us, I'd like to talk and reconsider other alternatives.")

These strategies may break the impasse. But what if none of these ideas work? What if the impasse is looking more and more like a permanent deadlock? At this point, some experts believe there's no further negotiation. If the other party will not budge and will not advance a persuasive basis for its position, then the conflict resolution process terminates.

With the Better End Strategy, we suggest five other options for you to try. Following is an example we recently observed that illustrates these alternatives.

An Impasse Example

A college-aged friend of ours, who's a new Christian, realized she had a conflict with the college minister of the church she attends. The staff member, who was originally very friendly and helpful in assisting her with some personal problems, suddenly and unpredictably turned a cold shoulder to her. Repeated efforts to reach him by phone led nowhere. Finally, she decided to write the following letter to him:

Dear Pastor _____,
It's important for me to communicate my feelings (fear, frustration, confusion, and anger) to you and to tell you what I would like from you.

Joining your college group has been a wonderful and enriching experience for me. When I first came to Heavenly Hills Chapel, before accepting Christ, the group was a powerful source of help for me. Everyone, including you, looked so happy and full of love—love for God and for others.

After receiving Jesus into my life and walking with Him a short time, I felt excited to be a member of your group. What a way for me as a new Christian to grow spiritually and encourage others to do so too! What a pleasure to meet you and your wife. As a result, I felt even more a part of the family of Christ.

Reaching out and trusting is very difficult for me because I've been so deeply hurt by my family since childhood. Meeting someone like you who really cared was a blessing. I believed you were concerned about me and my struggles and wanted to be as much a support as you could be.

Maybe I misinterpreted your messages. I really thought you wanted me to feel free to contact you when I needed a friend. I shared some of my recent struggles with you because I thought I could count on you.

Now I feel let down. You haven't responded to my notes or calls for the last two weeks. You seem reserved and businesslike when we pass each other at the church.

Maybe I'm asking too much from you! Too much time and support. Only you know if this is the case. Please tell me. Let me know if I'm asking for time which you do not have. Please don't leave it ambiguous for me. It's OK if you can't be there. If you know time and commitments are problems, I would like you to be honest and not offer them to me—or anyone else.

What I now feel is uneasiness around you. I find myself pulling away. I'm scared, and I'm concerned that I've asked too much from you and your wife.

After you read this, I hope we can meet to discuss it at your convenience. I really prayed about this letter before and while writing it. I hope you understand what I'm trying to say.

Well, I guess I've said enough for now. Thanks for listening (reading).

In Him,
Sandy

What an effort this person put into that letter! How she labored not to be offensive. How she aspired to be honest about her feelings and expectations as well as sensitive to his needs and limits. None of these steps worked.

After reading the letter, the pastor became unglued. He informed her she had overstepped the boundaries of decorum one last time. As far as he was concerned, he was no longer available to minister to her.

In this chapter, we address the question: What does she do next? The response she got was not what she expected—an unpleasant impasse with no apparent recourse. More pertinent to your negotiations, what can you do when you reach an apparent dead end like this one?

Throughout this book, we have challenged you to increase your motivation for and skill in resolving your intrapersonal, interpersonal, and organizational conflicts. We hope we've also stimulated you to help other people and organizations settle their disagreements more constructively.

The possibility that you'll be able to negotiate agreements to all your current and future disputes in ways that please God, yourself, and your adversaries won't only be difficult to implement, but it will be downright unlikely. At the same time, we want you to do all you can to be certain the impasse can't be overcome. Following are the five options you can explore when facing such a situation:

- *Incubation*—commit the conflict to God and wait;
- *Adaptation*—recognize and accept your opponent for who she or he is; tolerate and work around your differences;
- *Separation*—remove yourself, at least temporarily, from the intellectual, emotional, or physical influence of your opponent;
- *Mediation*—let a third party facilitate the negotiation;
- *Arbitration*—submit the dispute to a third party for a totally independent settlement.

Incubation

Sometimes when you've done your best (and you know it), the most desirable option is to recognize your inability to resolve the conflict, admit it, and then stop right there. Next, in prayer, turn the conflict over to God and wait for an answer. You opponent might even consent to join you in such a prayer for God's intervention in the issue. Meanwhile, go on with your life while watching for signs of change in the impasse.

This option entails one of Brian's most challenging developmental tasks—waiting! He has always revered persistence and follow-through. Stepping back and waiting for a situation to change, conditions to improve, storm clouds to break, and God to work aren't habits in his repertoire. But that doesn't mean he isn't working on changing such patterns!

We're not knocking the importance of persistence. As we mentioned earlier, too many people aren't tenacious enough in their conflict resolution efforts. We think the continuing saga of alarming rates of divorce and family separation in North America is partly due to individuals' giving up too soon.

Cohen (1980) favors a combination of patience and persistence, writing, "With the passage of sufficient time and repeated efforts on your part, almost every 'no' can be transformed into a 'maybe' and eventually a 'yes.' If you

allow a sufficient period for acceptance time and can fur-
nish them with the new information that they have not
considered in formulating their initial 'no,' you can win them
over" (p. 105).

At the same time, you'll encounter instances when persistence on your part isn't enough. Treat those as opportunities to follow David's advice: "Wait for the Lord; be strong,
and let your heart take courage; yes, wait for the Lord" (Ps.
27:14).

It's very possible that the Holy Spirit will produce the new
information required: a change in needs, feelings, expectations, or some new and creative Better End settlement for
you and your adversary.

If our despondent friend used the *incubation* option with
the minister of her church, she would back off, pray for
God's intervention and discernment in both of their lives,
and observe what transpired with the passage of time.

Adaptation
At times, you'll probably face impasses with individuals who
make it very difficult to find a resolution. Here are some
examples of behaviors that could prove frustrating and dis-
couraging to you. These individuals:

- preach or "speak at" you during the discussion;
- seldom change their minds once a decision is made;
- insist on having things their way even though other people get hurt;
- leave the room without "permission," ignore requests, or
  change the subject if an impasse occurs;
- like to force people to admit they've made a mistake;
- never admit they're wrong;
- never submit with pleasure.

There will also be times when you face impasses with
even more uncooperative individuals. Joyce Landorf calls
them "irregular people" (1982). Another popular author,
Robert Bramson (1981), terms them just plain "difficult."

You need an "attitude check" if you persist in negotiations with them. Unless these individuals are willing to negotiate, those conflicts won't get resolved in a meaningful

way that honors God and also addresses your feelings, needs, expectations, and limits.

These people could be:

- committed to saying "Yes, but..." when a possible settlement approaches.
- locked into faultfinding, blaming, or complaining;
- prone to chronic cheating and lying;
- overwhelmed by the need to "rescue" other people, consistently denying and ignoring their own needs;
- committed to bearing the label "victim" (bound by learned helplessness and "poor me" patterns);
- addicted to alcohol or drugs;
- determined to bully, attack, or otherwise emotionally abuse others;
- habituated to patterns of sexually or physically abusing other people;
- possessed or oppressed by evil spirits;

Can you add any examples to this list of unhealthy behavior patterns? Maybe we should discourage you from doing that for long—or else there won't be anyone left with whom to negotiate! Happily, we're convinced that a relatively small portion of the people we meet show such difficult tendencies. At the same time, we recommend that you prepare to encounter such people at the negotiating tables of your life.

So what? What can you do when that occurs? Consider the following suggestions, add to them, and allow the *adaptation* approach with which you feel most comfortable to evolve.

- Try some of the responses we suggest in chapters 6 and 9.
- Adapt your awareness by recognizing and labeling your opponent's recurring actions.
- Recognize what, if anything, you're adding to the situation by your behavior and lack of skills.
- Adapt your thinking; admit to yourself that the other person has a problem and recognize you don't have to become a therapist to solve that impediment.
- Ask God to work in that person's life.

■ Adapt your behavior by withdrawing gracefully while agreeing to disagree with the other person.
■ Get on with other activities in your own life.
■ Resist any temptation to return to the negotiation process before you see evidence that the other person has solved, or made significant progress on, his or her prevailing problem.
■ Consider using *mediation* or *arbitration*, as described below.

It was tempting for our friend to label not just the actions but the personality of the college minister. Terms like "Minister of Noncaring" and "Phony" went through her mind for a while.

But somehow she couldn't resign herself to categorizing him as a "difficult" or "irregular" person. She preferred to concentrate not on his personality or life patterns, but rather on what she believed was a specific communication problem between them.

Separation

Knowing when to walk away is a key skill for your negotiating repertoire. If and when you do this, however, we strongly recommend that *you get your adversary's explicit agreement on using the step.*

In the previous option, *adaptation*, the probability of continuing the negotiation to a fruitful settlement is low. With *separation*, provided the option is used correctly, the possibility is high. Frequently, you'll find that some emotional and physical distance between you and your opponent is necessary for a constructive interval.

Even Christ used the *separation* option as a means of dealing with a conflict. When people in the synagogue responded in rage over His confrontative remarks, He withdrew from Nazareth saying, "Truly I say to you, no prophet is welcome in his home town" (Luke 4:24). He apparently concluded that it was time for Him to depart.

Jesus terminated discussions with the Pharisees and the chief priests when they clearly rejected His message and were trying to trap Him in mental games. He used the *sepa-*

ration option at least these two times:

> And leaving them, He again embarked and went away to the other side (Mark 8:13).

> Jesus therefore no longer continued to walk publicly among the Jews, but went away from there to the country (John 11:54).

It's amazing to realize that, though Christ knew the hearts of those Jewish leaders, He repeatedly chose to attempt conflict resolution with them throughout His time on earth. He periodically separated from them, only to return later— giving them another chance to accept His words.

Separation can take several forms and can vary from nonconstructive to beneficial. Let's examine the differences, starting with the nonconstructive.

Samuel Vuchinich (1985) studied four methods used to handle arguments. Two of the four involved the *separation* option. He called those two "withdrawal" and "standoff." Actual physical separation, which he called *withdrawal,* was used least often of the four tactics. In this case, one party actually left the room or the residence.

Standoff was the prevalent approach. Members would remain in the same room but simply refuse to talk or otherwise interact with each other. "Many times another family member intervened and introduced a new topic or made a joke to try to cool off the conflict" (p. 43).

Vuchinich concludes that standoffs are undesirable, especially in marital and family conflicts, "If conflicts are frequent and standoffs are the usual way of ending them, frustration and animosity are likely to develop" (p. 46). We agree that standoffs are nonproductive and don't recommend them to you as a resolution strategy.

In contrast, *mutually agreeable, structured separations* can be very constructive when other options haven't worked and cooling-off periods are necessary. These planned separations can take different forms.

Some disputing couples and families are coached to use

the *separation* option while continuing to live under the same roof. David Mace (1985) calls this "coexistence" and states that the parties must make "an agreement to differ, at least for the time being" (p. 57). For a predetermined time, the people coexist in the same house while sharply curtailing their discussion of issues which they can't resolve. Ideally, they have regularly scheduled counseling sessions in order to deal with feelings and issues.

In the more common type of structured separation, the opponents live in different residences. However, the physical and emotional distance can make it difficult for them to reinitiate their negotiations. *That's why separate-residence separations should be considered only as "last-ditch" alternatives in marriage or family conflict.*

If you're facing this type of separation, we encourage you to proceed prayerfully, cautiously, and compassionately. Be certain that this is a well-structured, time-limited experiment. Carefully draw up a written "constructive separation" plan, designed around measurable objectives for what the two sides want to accomplish by the separation, and then stick with it.

For further assistance, read the helpful book, *Hope for the Separated* (1982) by Gary Chapman. He offers some excellent suggestions. We encourage you to try his strategies for healing damaged relationships.

After reeling from the college minister's unexpected barrage, our friend considered dropping her membership in Heavenly Hills Chapel. She also thought about calling the minister to see if he'd agree to her taking a "leave of absence" for a defined time period. But she saw both of these steps as withdrawal and conflict avoidance on her part. Since she wasn't able to get his participation in any kind of "structured separation," she decided to look for another option.

Mediation

This option makes use of a person called a "mediator," an individual who is called in by you and your opponent to help you settle your conflict. According to *The New Bible Dic-*

tionary (1962), the function of a mediator is "to intervene between two parties in order to promote relations between them which the parties themselves are not able to effect" (p. 802).

When employing this option, you and your opponent agree to use this supposedly objective ("disinterested") third party to continue negotiations with you. When you agree to this option, you commit yourselves to follow through by cooperatively participating in the mediated discussions and decisions.

Typically in North American culture, lawyers and union representatives perform this mediator role in interpersonal, intraorganizational, and interorganizational conflicts. Other people, such as ministers, psychologists, managers, and friends, can and do perform this role, however.

Mediators were common throughout biblical times. In the Old Testament, priests often performed a mediatory function. "Then the priests, the sons of Levi, shall come near, for the Lord your God has chosen them to serve Him and to bless in the name of the Lord; and every dispute and every assault shall be settled by them" (Deut. 21:5).

At the same time, priests weren't the only mediators. For example, Moses was a mediator *par excellence*. Not only did he mediate in disputes among people to the point of exhaustion (Deut. 1:9-13). He also was the mediator between God and man by receiving the Law and giving it to the people.

Jonathan, Saul's son, attempted to negotiate a settlement between his father and David. That difficult conflict was intensified by Saul's intense jealousy of David and deep bitterness (1 Sam. 19:1-7).

In the New Testament, Jesus provides a classic example of a mediator in action. The Pharisees, anxious for a stoning and again hoping to trap Christ, brought Him a woman accused of adultery. The Evangelist John recorded the scene, "But when they persisted in asking Him, He straightened up, and said to them, 'He who is without sin among you, let him be the first to throw a stone at her.' And when they heard it, they began to go out one by one, beginning with the older ones, and He was left alone, and the woman, where she had been, in the midst" (John 8:7, 9).

Even more spectacular is history's most wondrous illustration of *mediation:* Christ's intervention with God on our behalf. "For there is one God, and one mediator also between God and men, the Man Christ Jesus" (1 Tim. 2:5). Jesus is the ultimate mediator. In His life He modeled reconciliation; in His death He effected a substitutionary atonement that covered His people's sin. And as the resurrected Christ sits at the right hand of God, He continues to intercede with God on our behalf.

The Bible also provides guidelines for the mediation of conflicts between us and our earthly opponents. Look at how the words of Jesus speak directly to the issue of conflict resolution. "And if your brother sins, go and reprove him in private; if he listens to you, you have won your brother. But if he does not listen to you, take one or two more with you, so that by the mouth of two or three witnesses every fact may be confirmed. And if he refuses to listen to them, tell it to the church, and if he refuses to listen even to the church, let him be to you as a Gentile and a tax-gatherer" (Matt. 18:15-17).

That's a series of direct and powerful mediation steps. This passage (and the Better End Strategy) encourage you to first try to resolve your conflicts directly with your adversaries. You involve other people at increasing levels of authority only if your initial attempts fail.

To illustrate an advanced application of the *mediation* option, we direct your attention to the Christian Conciliation Service, a ministry of the Christian Legal Society. This service (see Resources listing for information) does the following:

■ Distributes educational materials which promote an increasing recognition of the need for Christians to find alternatives to the traditional adversary structures of lawsuits.

■ Provides (for specific disputes) materials explaining the commitment to mediation as a biblical means of dispute resolution and steps in implementing such a process.

- Identifies a number of persons who are willing to serve as mediators and who possess the requisite skills and commitments.
- Maintains an administrative office which selects a mediator, arranges for a hearing, and otherwise assists in implementing a commitment by parties to utilize this service.

Procedures used by the Christian Conciliation Service are less formal than those of the judicial court system. Fortunately, there is less emphasis on adversarial proceedings. Parties may be represented by counsel. However, the procedures are designed to be less "technical." According to this service, such a process often provides more opportunity for reconciliation, is less costly, and consumes less time than do lawsuits. Its essential difference, however, is the inclusion of a vital spiritual dimension.

If you decide that the *mediation* option is appropriate for the impasse or deadlock you and another party are experiencing, or if you are asked to play the mediator role in someone else's conflict, here are a few suggestions that could help the process:

- Carefully select the people who will attend the meeting. Be cautious about adding anyone in addition to the two parties. "The fewer the better" is a safe adage here.
- Agree with the mediator on your desired outcomes— what you'd like to leave the mediation meeting with.
- Agree with the mediator on a tentative agenda for the meeting.
- As a group, write down the desired outcomes and proposed agenda.
- Develop a physical signal system with the mediator to keep the meeting moving smoothly. (For example, a raised hand could mean, "I'd like to go over that point again.")
- Help the mediator establish ground rules to make the meeting successful.
- Keep using the skills you learned for one-on-one negotiation in chapters 5 and 6.

If you ever agree to serve as a mediator in someone's dispute, you'll have a prime opportunity to test your listening skills because that will be one of your major challenges. Besides carefully listening to and summarizing what each side says, you'll try to stimulate their creative problem-solving. You'll also suggest areas on which they agree—the base on which we recommend you always build—and areas on which each side can compromise or come up with a new, creative solution.

Throughout the mediation process, take opportunities to encourage each opponent, not only for their effective communication skills, but also to consider trying new ones.

If you can be used to help individuals resolve the issues over which they're at odds, you'll perform a gratifying service. If you're able to facilitate their reconciliation, you'll experience one of the best natural highs you've ever had. God can use you mightily this way in people's lives.

That's the way He used another staff member who helped our college friend and her minister opponent work through their impasse.

Arbitration
In both the *mediation* and *arbitration* options, you and your opponent turn to a third party to help work through an impasse. In *mediation*, you and your opponent(s) continue to meet but with a mediator present. The *arbitration* option requires that each of you meets separately with the arbitrator. The arbitrator then comes up with solutions.

Typically, the arbitrator follows a procedure such as the following:

- establishes ground rules for the arbitration process;
- identifies the issues over which there is conflict;
- listens to each of the opposing parties;
- takes a time period to consider the opposing arguments;
- obtains additional help from other experts or documents;
- renders a decision.

In *The Art of Negotiating* (1968) Nierenberg asserts one of the primary benefits of the *arbitration* option. He's convinced that it's face-saving for each side to talk separately with a third, neutral party. Each opponent then finds it more palatable to grant concessions to the arbitrator, rather than directly to his or her opponent.

To the two of us, a more important benefit is the product that results from the typical arbitration outlined above. You and your adversary agree to settle. Your impasse is broken because that's the key condition with which you had to agree when you selected this type of *arbitration* option.

You and the other party promised to accept the arbitrator's decision as final and enforceable. Therefore, in agreeing to use this variation of *arbitration*, both parties are saying settlement is wanted. It will be accepted. Subsequently, you both must act as though the settlement is binding. Voilà! Your deadlock disappears.

A variation of the *arbitration* option requires a less stringent initial agreement between you and your opponent. Here, you both agree to treat the arbitrator's conclusion only as a recommendation.

You might choose this option if you and your opponent have a history of successful conflict resolutions together, but you'd like another opinion this time. Or you might agree to use this option if both parties believe settlement is desirable—but unlikely. A third party's opinion might shed new light on the issues.

You agree to treat the arbitrator's decision as advisory, and one (or both) of you is free to accept or reject its content. If rejection occurs, you're back to Impasse—with a capital "I." This chapter's other four options or the first *arbitration* variation are your next alternatives.

Currently in the United States, professional sports provides one of the most commonly recognized examples of the *arbitration* option. These instances seem to get more attention than do some of our Supreme Court decisions.

Take baseball, for example. If a player reaches an impasse with his club owner over a conflict involving salary and/or other benefits, under certain circumstances he can request arbitration. If the owner approves, they agree to accept the decision of a hired third party. Using what's called "final offer arbitration," each side submits offers, and the arbitrator chooses one.

The arbitrator does not select a compromise between the two. Each side tries to come close, in making its final offer, to what it predicts the arbitrator will estimate as fair. If a player or his agent overestimates his worth, he could lose considerably by having to accept his club owner's offer.

In the impasse dropped on our college friend, she decided against the *arbitration* option. She wanted to meet with the college minister face-to-face with the help of a mediator. Even though the conflict was upsetting her, she still didn't believe it was serious enough to recommend turning it over to someone else.

These are the strategies we recommend when all else fails. Before you go on to learn ways of handling unfair tactics, try the next two experiments.

Experiment 15: "Difficult Impasses"

A. Recall and analyze at least one *personal* and one *organizational* impasse you've recently faced.

B. For each one, answer the following questions.

	Personal Impasse	Organizational Impasse
1. What did you do that caused the impasse?		
2. What do you think your opponent did that caused the impasse?		
3. What impact did the result have on you?		
4. What was the impact on your opponent?		
5. How would you like to handle that type of impasse the next time you face it?		

C. Discuss your responses with someone who could be helpful (maybe each opponent).

Experiment 16: "Dreaded Opponents"

A. Identify the characteristics of three different people with whom you dread having a conflict and reaching an impasse.
B. In the left column below, use a few key words to describe each characteristic.
C. In the right column, summarize at least one thing you want to do in the future to avoid reacting in your typical style with that person.

Person's Characteristics	*Improvements You'll Try in Future Impasses with Him/Her*

Person #1

   (e.g., very talkative)   _____

_____   _____

_____   _____

Person #2

_____   _____

_____   _____

_____   _____

Person #3

_____   _____

_____   _____

_____   _____

D. Discuss your responses with someone else more practiced in conflict resolution skills.

CHAPTER NINE

Don't Be Naive: Recognizing and Handling Unfair Tactics

Conduct yourself with wisdom toward outsiders, making the most of the opportunity.

—*Colossians 4:5*

With the BEST, you now know a fair and principled approach to resolve conflicts. You could stop at this point in your learning and refuse to negotiate with anyone who doesn't use a similar approach. Although that stance may be tempting, we think it's also naive. We don't recommend it for several reasons.

First of all, we believe God wants us to be fair and giving, but He doesn't want us to be fools in our interactions with our opponents. He expects us to use our knowledge and skills. One of the most powerful messages we can give to others is the fact that we are bright, aware, and competent individuals.

Second, as we mention early in this book, most people haven't had training in the Better End Strategy or similar methods of resolving conflicts in which all parties are fairly treated as well as satisfied with the results. Consequently, most of the opponents you meet will make it very difficult for you to use your well-organized, firm-yet-fair approach. Without necessarily meaning to be cruel, they'll use tactics that are actually unfair to you—and maybe even offensive to God. Be aware of those tactics, and then be better prepared.

Third, another group of your opponents may purposely use unfair, deceptive tactics in order to take advantage of your fairness or perceived naïveté. The more aware you are of these "tricks," the more you'll be able to stand up to them and defend yourself—not with equally devious tactics, but with *fair and principled countertactics*.

In this chapter, we describe some of the most common and important negotiation tactics you may encounter. Though most of these can occur at any time, we group them into three sets according to whether they're likely to appear at the beginning of the resolution process, anytime during your interactions, or near the end (or even after) reaching a settlement. For each ploy, we offer some suggestions on how you might handle it.

Tricks in the Early Stages
You may encounter the following techniques during the time you're preparing for a formal resolution meeting or during the initial stage of the actual meeting itself.

■ *Total Refusal to Negotiate.* Despite several invitations to participate in the resolution process, your opponent may continue to refuse to talk with you about the issues. He or she may laugh off your requests, try to change the subject, or suggest that the issues "aren't really important." Your adversary may even become rude and angry, threatening you if you continue to "nag." You're faced with an "avoider" who has no intentions of negotiating.

What You Can Do: Don't give up too early. Give your opponent several opportunities to respond, offering times and places that you know are convenient. Be patient and pleasant, while still conveying how important the issues are to you.

If the party still refuses to cooperate, ask him or her for the principle underlying this position. Convey the idea that you know the individual is fair and principled, and that you want to understand his or her underlying value or logic. This often forces the person to recognize any unfairness and to move toward more cooperation. (Remember, most people think of themselves as fair, honest, and principled.)

If this doesn't work, you have some additional choices. You can state that, unless you hear to the contrary, you're going to proceed as if the agreement you desire has been accepted. ("Since you aren't willing to discuss my returning to graduate school, I'm going to assume that you approve of my plan. I'll register next Wednesday and be in classes every Tuesday and Thursday evenings.")

Another strategy is to call in a third party to approach and try to negotiate on your behalf with your opponent. Here you'd use either the *mediation* or *arbitration* options from chapter 8. Finally, you can postpone discussions indefinitely, submitting the conflict to God in the *incubation* option, or you can decide to submit with pleasure to your opponent's needs.

■ *Resistance.* This tactic differs from a total refusal to negotiate, though in some ways it looks the same. The ploy is usually used in a buying-selling context. Despite a physical presence at the "negotiating table," the other party pretends to be disinterested in what you have to offer.

For example, you're showing your house to a prospective buyer. The person says some variation of this, "To tell you the truth, my spouse and I aren't really interested in buying right now. We're just out for a Sunday drive and thought we'd take a look."

Despite the fact that he and his wife have driven 25 miles up a steep mountain, in the pouring rain, to see the place, and you've spotted them murmuring and exchanging excited glances as they look around the property, he claims total disinterest, even boredom with the whole situation.

What You Can Do: Don't argue or point out the signs that indicate the person may be bluffing. Assume the resistance is probably a ploy, but respond as if it's the truth. Then see if you can still provide additional information. ("I understand you're not really interested in what I'm offering. In case you decide to reconsider later or might know someone else that could want it, may I just mention a few key features that aren't apparent, as well as the reasonable price I'm asking?")

You can also take the person at his or her word, and start to pull away or end the discussion. This gentle "bluff calling" should quickly reveal your opponent's true intent.

■ *"I Want It All."* Your opponent may open up the negotiation with very extreme demands: a very high (or low) price, totally unrealistic time limits or deadlines, or some other outrageous offer. Many negotiators purposely start with what they know to be unreasonable requests, knowing that they must and will settle for less in the bargaining. What's amazing is that some people don't realize the requests are unreasonable, and accept them!

What You Can Do: Be sure you do your homework before entering the negotiation. Have in mind the maximums and minimums you'll accept. Know your BATNA so that you can say no, if appropriate, and won't be taken off guard in the meeting.

As a rule of thumb, don't accept first offers. If the suggestion is totally preposterous, show that you're aware of this, perhaps even calling it a joke on your opponent's part. ("Good for you in proposing such an outrageous opening gambit! You've helped me stretch my thinking about how high/low I'd really like to go. That can only help us come up with a really fair and solid final agreement.")

If your opponent's idea sounds somewhat but not totally reasonable, make a note of the proposal, and ask for some time to consider it. Even when an early offer sounds quite attractive, it's usually to everyone's advantage to wait until additional alternatives are discussed before a settlement is made.

■ *"Low Balling."* This is another tactic often found in the sales arena (especially car sales), though it can appear in other negotiations as well. The tactic is a variation of the "I-Want-It-All" approach, though it is even more devious because your adversary uses outright deception in the proposal.

A seller offers you a very desirable price, one that's far better than that of any of the other sellers. This extreme offer causes you to eliminate the other competitors. Once you and the seller come to agreement, she announces that the price will actually be much higher because of some "extras." By then the competitors have made other commitments, and either you're stuck with the new price, or else you have to start your search all over.

What You Can Do: Don't wait until the last minute to negotiate important issues. Allow some backup time in anticipation of such ploys. As usual, know your BATNA, and be sure that you have at least one and preferably more equally good alternatives to the proposed offer.

Be suspicious of proposals that are extremely different from the rest of the offers. Get bids with their effective time periods in writing, and report illegal or unethical practices to authorities. Refuse to negotiate in the future with these unprincipled opponents.

■ *Time Investment.* Without your realizing it, the other party may draw you toward a commitment by getting you to increase your time investments. Before you know what's happening, you've accepted an idea that you may not have agreed to had the idea been presented to you "cold."

First, you read a notice (not much time involved); then you return a short questionnaire (still not much effort, you think). Next, you have a short chat on the phone and agree to a brief meeting ("Just to pick your brain"). Before you know it, you find yourself agreeing to be the director of your church's fundraising program—at the same time you're working overtime at your job, taking care of your ailing mother, coaching Little League, and recovering from a major rejection in your life!

What You Can Do: Don't automatically agree to all requests for your time. Know what your needs and priorities are, and ask yourself, "Is this a good use of my time?" Recognize what's happening if the other party begins to ask for a series of "small things" from you.

State your limits early enough so the other person isn't shocked when you refuse the ultimate offer ("I'm more than happy to return the questionnaire. This is an extremely busy time for me, so that's all I'll be able to contribute to the program this winter.") Being honest in this way will prevent misunderstandings and resentments on both sides.

■ *Deadlines.* Your opponents can use at least two deadline tactics. First, they can press you to reveal a deadline you're facing. Once they know your time constraints, they can delay any serious negotiating until the last moment, forcing you into concessions you probably would have avoided if given more time.

Your opponents can also claim phony deadlines on their side. If you don't accept their proposal by such-and-such time, it will be "too late."

What You Can Do: Try not to reveal your schedule, if you have one in mind. Almost all deadlines, including yours, are negotiable; so go into the meeting with a flexible attitude. Take the time you need to research options, weigh proposals, and make decisions.

If you're suspicious of your opponent's stated deadline, try to find out how real it is. Check with other knowledgeable people, if necessary. Again, most deadlines are negotiable. You can catch a later flight, ask the agency for an extension, pay the baby-sitter to stay longer, or otherwise buy more time to think through strategies and evaluate your options.

■ *Exaggerating Small Concessions.* If your opponent is an experienced negotiator, he or she will probably make a big deal out of every concession offered to you. The hypothesis is that the more you regard each concession as a major sacrifice, the more you'll be willing to "give" on an issue of genuine importance to your opponent.

This is a tactic often used by authorities when negotiating with terrorists over hostages. Every single request of the terrorists is discussed and pondered at length. Even the smallest demand, such as type of food and drinks to be sent in, is debated, exaggerated, analyzed, and negotiated at length so that the terrorists are convinced they're "winning" a major point.

What You Can Do: Set your own "importance value" on your requests. If it's a small thing you're asking, say so, and be willing to drop the request if it becomes a manipulative point. Watch the time, and suggest that you postpone an issue until later if your opponent is purposely dragging on a decision. Pursue your important requests, and don't think you must sacrifice what's important just because your opponent conceded something to you.

■ *Trial Balloon.* Your opponent may, early in the negotiations, toss out a proposed solution in order to test your receptivity to it. ("I realize we're nowhere near a solution on this, but just for fun, if I were to offer you _____, what would be your first reaction?") The U.S. government often does this to test public opinion on various strategies it's considering.

Your opponent isn't entirely joking. Generally, the person is revealing something he or she really supports. Once you give your reaction, your adversary can come up with a revised solution or develop a strategy to sell you on this one.

What You Can Do: Use the information within the "balloon" to help determine your negotiating range with this person. Does this match the information you gathered prior to the meeting? Or does this signal some new flexibility or rigidity on your adversary's part? Even if the hypothetical offer sounds quite attractive, delay your opinion and suggest that you both take some time to consider it—as well as other alternatives.

Tricks to Watch for in the Negotiation Process
Watch for the following tactics throughout your conflict resolution meetings.
■ *The Flinch.* A "flinch" is a visible reaction to a remark or proposal you make. It could be a dramatic facial expression, such as widened eyes, raised eyebrows, or a mouth that drops open. It could be a sudden movement backward

(as if ducking a punch) or an abrupt remark such as "What?" "You're kidding!" or "No way!"

Your opponent may use a flinch to register actual or feigned shock, disgust, or disbelief. The purpose is to try to make you feel ridiculous for saying what you did.

What You Can Do: Recognize the flinch for what it is, a dramatic ploy. You can comment as though you believe the gesture ("I see you're surprised by my remark") was meant to invite the sharing of more helpful information. On the other hand, if this is a common, exaggerated reaction for your opponent, ignore it and continue on with your proposal.

■ *The Hot Potato.* In the middle of your negotiations, your opponent may reveal a problem he faces and throw it into your lap to get you to solve it. The intent is to disrupt the orderly flow of the discussion and try for a hasty concession on your part.

For example, your teenager asks to talk about her possible use of the family car next weekend. Since you and your spouse need it for your usual Friday night square dancing class, you offer the vehicle for Saturday night. Your daughter suddenly says, "But I've already promised my friends that I'd drive them to the game Friday night." She's consciously or unconsciously thrown a constraint which she's created to you, expecting it to force a settlement of the problem her way.

Other opponents will bring up deadlines, shortages of items, lack of staff, their lack of profit, or other problems in an effort to talk you into their solutions.

What You Can Do: If the problem is a legitimate one and you sense the other party is being equitable, we know you'll want to be fair in return. We encourage you to be flexible and reasonable, even sacrificing your needs from time to time for the sake of maintaining strong relationships.

At the same time, if this is a pattern in your opponent's behavior, or if the problem is the result of an immoral or selfish action, we suggest you toss the potato back. Let the other side solve the problem and live with the consequences.

■ *Intimidation.* Your opponent can try to intimidate you in numerous ways, including criticizing you unfairly or attacking you with words or even actions. A more subtle form of intimidation is criticism or challenges related to your faith. "I thought Christians were kind and forgiving" or "The Bible says . . ."

What You Can Do: Your first countertactic is to realize what your opponent is attempting to do—trying to make you feel weak and less powerful than he or she is. Chapter 6 presented several strategies for handling these objections and oral attacks by your opponents. Study and practice these suggestions to be well prepared for any "emotional button pushing" your adversaries may try.

■ *The Vise.* This tactic is commonly used by skilled negotiators; in fact, it's almost expected. In response to a proposal you offer, your opponent says, "You'll have to do better than that."

What You Can Do: Respond by fishing for more information: "And just how much better do I have to do?" Listen carefully for additional facts about how high or low your opponent may be willing to go.

■ *Fait Accompli.* This tactic may shock you a little, as it does the two of us every time we run into it. Your opponent, while pretending to be in a negotiation, goes ahead and does exactly what he or she wants to do without agreement from you. For example, while you and your neighbor are in the courts battling over his proposed chicken coop and egg stand, he goes ahead and builds the coop, buys the chickens, and starts selling the eggs! Preposterous? Yes, and it's done all the time.

Your opponent may take the large risk of implementing the desired option without your approval in the hope that the eventual ruling will support it. The old adage "It's easier to ask forgiveness than ask permission" applies here. Since enforcement agencies take a long time to act, and since most of us are polite and don't retaliate, people get away with such wrongful maneuvers.

What You Can Do: Sometimes there is very little you can do to stop your opponent from taking action. We recommend that you try at least the following. Express your disappointment and dissatisfaction with the actions, preferably in person, with a mediator if necessary. If you say nothing, your opponent will think silence is acceptance.

Go on record opposing the action. Keep an informal diary or log of exactly what you tried to do and when, plus the response. You may be called on to produce this later. Write a letter to the individual stating your displeasure and, if appropriate, send a copy to the suitable agency.

Refuse to provide your part of the settlement, if anything is expected. Again, go on record explaining why. Rally others around your cause. Take legal steps, if necessary, to prevent further actions.

Finally, closely monitor your needs and desired outcomes regarding this issue. Is it less important to you now? Is fighting this action taking too much of your time, dishonoring God, or hurting other people? If so, consider submitting with pleasure on the issue.

■ *Telephone Tricks.* Your opponent can use the telephone as a way of taking advantage of you. By being caught off guard, you may be talked into concessions you'll regret later.

Since you'll probably feel pressure to be brief on the telephone, you won't explore issues as deeply or carefully as you would in person. Because the discussion is briefer, there is more risk of misunderstanding. It's also easier for your adversary to say no to your requests when not faced with the prospect of looking you in the eye.

What You Can Do: As a general rule, try not to negotiate on the phone, particularly when you stand to lose more than the other party does. If you must use the phone, don't negotiate until you've had a chance to prepare. Wait until you have sufficient time to talk.

Treat the call as you would an in-person meeting. Take the time to set up an agenda and ground rules. Listen very carefully because you won't have the visual clues to help you. Also, offer to write the draft of the final settlement so that you can include your interpretations of the resolution.

Tricks close to or after the Finish Line

These final tactics are ones you're likely to see in the final minutes of your conflict resolution meetings—or sometime after the meetings end.

■ *Good Guy/Bad Guy.* If you and the other side are having difficulty settling on an issue, such as final price, you may run into this unfair tactic. Here's how it typically goes. One member of the opposing side makes you an unrealistic offer. Just as expected, you refuse to accept this solution. Since the offer is so unreasonable, you're probably somewhat upset and insulted. The "bad guy" then leaves the meeting under the ·pretense of giving up because of your stubbornness.

At this point, a second person from the opposing side appears, apologizing for the "rude" or "unreasonable" behavior of his partner. This "good guy" then presents *the same or only slightly better offer* to you. You're placated by the apology and grateful for this new "concession" and thus agree to the settlement.

What You Can Do: First of all, don't assume the "good guy" is on your side, as he would have you believe. Be polite, yet firm, as you refuse to concede until the proposal meets your criteria. Suggest that the "bad guy" join you again for the rest of the negotiation. Treat the situation like the "hot potato" mentioned above, letting the two opposing team members solve the supposed problem.

■ *Small-Increment Bids.* An experienced opponent knows that it's smart to inch slowly, not quickly, toward a final settlement. For example, if you're asking $200 for your used television, your opponent may bid $150, then $155, and $157.50 rather than jumping by fives or tens (the way beginning negotiators would do). As this is going on, you'll probably feel pressure to move much closer to the low bid.

What You Can Do: Be realistic in the first place about your asking price. Check ads for similar items or services to be certain you're requesting a fair amount. Once the bargaining begins, resist the urge to drop your price immediately down near to your opponent's bid. If you decide to drop down, you can drop in similar small increments ($195,

$190, $187.50). You can then continue to inch toward the final goal. Concede gradually in similar situations where you are faced with offers far from your desired target.

■ *Higher Authority.* A common ploy, even in international negotiations, is the use of the Higher (or Limited) Authority tactic. You and your opponent move through the negotiation, hammering out a final settlement. You may find that you've conceded quite a bit in your final offer in order to get the other party to agree.

Just when you think you have a deal, the members of the other side tell you they can't give you a final "yes." They confess that it will be necessary to bounce the proposal off some higher authority—a spouse, partner, boss, or board of directors. This higher authority then treats your proposal not as the final settlement but as *the starting point of a second (the "official") negotiation!*

What You Can Do: Check out the decision-making authority of the other party very early in the meeting. Say something like this: "If we can come to some agreement today, is there any reason you can't give final approval for our settlement?"

If you learn that indeed your opponents won't make the final decision, as is often the case, find out who will be the final authority. Make your proposals in such a way that you totally win over these people and make it easy for them to sell the idea to the top decision-maker. You might even suggest that you go to the higher authority together, so you can help provide essential information.

■ *The Nibble.* Let's assume you and your adversary have had a long discussion and have finally come to agreement on a key issue. You feel relieved that the negotiation is finally over. Don't be surprised if, at this point, he or she brings up new needs.

Unfair? Probably, but many opponents won't miss the chance to squeeze in several requests at the last minute. They gamble that you won't want to appear stingy or risk the entire deal on a few "small" extras. Thus, you're asked to throw in a tie with the new suit, a table with the used television, or Friday afternoon as part of a weekend you offered to spend with a friend.

What You Can Do: Tell the other party, "Yes, I would mind throwing in the _____. Our agreement is for _____." Let the person feel a little sheepish or embarrassed for asking for more. ("You've done such a great job of negotiating, and we have such a solid agreement. You're not going to ask me for more now, are you?")

Another tactic is to simply smile as if you've caught the person in a good joke. ("Oh, that's funny, George. You almost had me there for a moment. I love your sense of humor.") Or finally, treat the new request as another issue for negotiation and state your willingness to deal with it at a future time and place.

■ *Take It or Leave It.* Many of your opponents who haven't learned to negotiate fairly will use this statement as their automatic defense of any solution they offer. Since this is an ultimatum, it's a difficult tactic to handle, particularly if the stakes are very important to you.

What You Can Do: Your best strategy is to know your BATNA in advance of the discussion. How high, far, or low are you willing to go in the negotiation instead of turning to your alternative? Do you have a strong alternative? Have you prayed about the issue?

If after all this analysis you decide the proposal is worth taking, concede to your opponent's request. If you've done your homework well, you should have no real regrets about your decision. On the other hand, if accepting the terms would be worse than your BATNA, say no, walk away, and allow yourself to feel good about that—even when you've expended a great deal of time in the negotiation!

■ *Impasse or Deadlock on Purpose.* Your opponent may purposely throw obstacles in the way of any final agreements. He may do this by stalling, presenting outrageous demands, refusing to follow the ground rules, ignoring the agreement criteria you both supposedly set, withholding vital facts, lying, or otherwise causing serious impasses in your negotiations.

Your adversary may be doing this just to exercise power and force you into later concessions. He may have a more attractive BATNA and be trying to get you to end the negotiation—thus relieving him of any responsibility and guilt for terminating it.

What You Can Do: Be sure that you have a strong BATNA yourself, particularly when you enter negotiations with difficult opponents. Describe the behavior you observe without laying blame or attacking in return. Suggest process checks and time-outs when your opponent continues to obstruct the negotiation. Probe for hidden needs and reasons behind his or her comments and actions.

But remain strong and don't give in to these unreasonable tactics. Refuse to continue the process until your opponent is willing to cooperate. Consider using a mediator or arbitrator in your future encounters.

■ *Pseudosettlement.* We end with this unfair tactic because to us, it's the most frustrating of all. In the meeting, your opponent pretends to agree wholeheartedly with the settlement reached. Afterward, he or she doesn't carry out the commitments. At first a token effort might be made, but very soon the old behavior appears. It's as if the meeting and settlement never took place.

We see this tactic used all the time. Even when settlement documents are carefully drawn up and a strategy for monitoring progress in is place, some adversaries ignore and totally sabotage the entire arrangement. Others try to meet their commitments, but promises fall by the wayside when other priorities enter their lives.

What You Can Do: Expect some "postsettlement fallout" in all of the agreements you make with your adversaries. All of us are most enthusiastic about commitments when they're fresh. Plan to be somewhat flexible on your expectations and requirements.

At the same time, do what you can to retain the spirit of your agreements. Write down specifically what is to be done, by whom, and by when. Use a mediator to help both of you monitor progress. Set up progress meetings to formally check how things are going for both sides.

Give your opponent encouragement and other rewards for carrying out her commitments. These could be a few words of thanks and appreciation, even when the meeting is history and the behaviors are automatic. Rewards could be more tangible, in the form of notes, small gifts, or celebrations.

Finally, be sure to enforce the penalties built into the agreement when your opponent doesn't follow through. But don't use people caught in the middle, such as children, to carry out penalties. For instance, if your ex-spouse reneges on her agreement to take the children on an agreed-upon weekend, don't punish your "ex" or your children as well by refusing to allow them to go with her at the next visitation opportunity.

Final Thoughts on Unfair Tactics

Now that you've reviewed these tactics, you may be thinking of ways you could use a few of them in your own interpersonal relationships. How good it would feel to give your unfair opponents a taste of what it's like to be taken advantage of.

What we recommend as an alternative, however, is to run your desired reactions through the test proposed in *Getting to Yes*. Fisher and Ury suggest that you ask yourself, "Is this an approach I would use in dealing with a good friend or a member of my family? If a full account of what I said and did appeared in the newspapers, would I be embarrassed?" (p. 148) To that we add: When you're finally facing the Lord and He is examining your life and actions, would you want this episode included in that account?

We assume that you're much wiser now about what you'll face in your future conflicts. To check your knowledge related to unfair tactics, try the experiments below. Then go on to the next chapter which focuses on recovering from damaging conflicts.

Experiment 17. "That's Unfair!"

A. Recall two conflicts or negotiations in which people used unfair tactics on you.

B. Answer the following questions about these experiences.

	1st Experience	2nd Experience
What tactic(s) did the other person use?		
What feelings did you have at the time?		
How did you respond to the tactic(s)?		
What could you do if you encountered the same tactic(s) again?		

C. Discuss these experiences with someone who's experienced in negotiation.

Experiment 18: "What Would You Do?"
This experiment is designed to sharpen your skills in recognizing and counteracting tactics used on you by others.

A. Read the following hypothetical situations while pretending you're faced with resolving them.

B. For each situation, (1) identify the unfair tactic used by your imaginary opponent, and (2) state what you would do next.

   1. You're holding a garage sale to clear out a lot of the items you've collected over the years. You're excited because a customer is actually buying an ugly old chest you thought you'd never sell. As he's counting out his money, he casually says, "I don't suppose you'd mind throwing in that old chair as part of the deal." The chair is quite valuable.

   Tactic being used:
   What would you do next?

   2. For weeks, you've asked your relative to sit down to

talk about an important issue that bothers you. Every time you ask, she says, "No thanks. You're making a big deal out of nothing."

Tactic being used:
What would you do next?

3. You decide to hire a landscaping firm to redo your front and backyards. Four firms are fairly high in price; the fifth is much lower. Despite the low price, the bidder assures you she can do the same work for that amount. You hire the lowest bidder. Two weeks later, the winning company lets you know that some materials and plants have gone up in price, and the job will take much longer (and more money) than first estimated.

Tactic being used:
What would you do next?

4. At your request, you and your work colleague have a discussion on punctuality. After a long, but pleasant meeting in which both of you share your needs and wishes, she agrees to be on time for your meetings and clients, just as you requested. You agree to stop nagging about the time. The next two times you're to meet clients, however, she's her usual twenty minutes late with no explanation.

Tactic being used:
What would you do next?

C. Discuss your answers with a person more skilled than you in negotiation skills.

CHAPTER TEN

Healing the Effects of Damaging Conflicts

And be kind to one another, tenderhearted, forgiving each other, just as God in Christ also has forgiven you.
—*Ephesians 4:32*

The one who loves his brother abides in the light and there is no cause for stumbling in him. But the one who hates his brother is in the darkness and walks in the darkness, and does not know where he is going because the darkness has blinded his eyes.
—*1 John 2:10-11*

How much time do you need to identify a conflict in which you or someone close to you experienced a bitter, painful ending? We're guessing only seconds. Instead of producing the benefits we outlined in chapter 1, such conflicts seem to have the exact opposite results. These disputes hurt one or both parties deeply.

Harmful conflicts can also have damaging repercussions for other people who aren't the main adversaries but who are indirectly involved. These include children exposed to their parents' battles, separation, or divorce.

Incidents of damaging results are ones that condition all of us to be at least apprehensive when there's a sign of conflict, even when we're not directly involved in it. As we noted earlier, for some people the intensity of that fear can increase right up to panic and phobic levels.

Examples of Damaging Conflicts

The Apostle Paul challenges us to be kind, tenderhearted, and forgiving (Eph. 4:32). John encourages us to love each other and not stumble in our spiritual lives (1 John 2:10-11). When these biblical guidelines aren't followed in handling disagreements, predictably poor results occur.

Here are examples of four types of conflicts which can produce damaging results for one or both parties:

■ A temporary impasse expands into a deadlock that isn't resolved.

—You and your boss can't agree on your job performance. She says the issue can't be resolved until your next performance review, six months from now.

—Your daughter refused to keep the curfew to which she agreed two weeks ago. You can't accept her defiance.

■ One party reluctantly agrees to a settlement imposed by the other side but immediately experiences strong dissatisfaction.

—You agree to teach a Sunday School class even though you know you're overburdened. You explained that to the Christian education director, but to no avail. You're unhappy as you leave her office.

—You promise your parents you'll improve your grades. But at the same time, you hate yourself for lacking the study skills and habits to handle the academic work.

■ One party accepts a settlement but much later becomes dissatisfied with it.

—When a person abused you, he made you promise not to tell anyone or he'd stop loving you. Now you're 11 years older and grieved that you ever accepted that bargain.

—One of your employees appeared to agree with your changing her job assignment. Over the last two months, however, her work products have deteriorated. You've

heard that she strongly dislikes her job—and you.
- Both sides painfully agree to a settlement.
  —Your union representatives hammer out a fringe benefits settlement that's reluctantly ratified by you, your
  colleagues, and your employer.
  —You and your ex-spouse struggle through the resolution of child custody privileges. As time goes on, both of
  you are unhappy with the results.

All of the above types of conflict produce pain—in you as
well as others. Your pain can vary from mild hurt and frustration to intense resentment and bitterness which can easily sour into deep hatred. What do you do with that emotional load? We strongly ecnourage you to take some important
steps.

We trust that you'll work through the pain, first by taking
constructive steps to heal it, and second by systematically
reducing the effects of the painful memories. In the remain-
der of this chapter, we will summarize five methods of heal-
ing the hurt from poorly handled or unresolved conflicts.
We recommend you use all of the following:
- Acknowledging the pain
- Valuing forgiveness
- Seeking forgiveness from opponents
- Forgiving opponents
- Fading the memories of damaging conflicts

**Healing Method 1: Acknowledging the Pain from Dam-
aging Conflicts**
Think of a deadlock you had with an unfair, difficult, or
unprincipled adversary. Was it a personal dispute? How
about a professional one?

Did you feel hurt from it? Perhaps because negotiating
was unpleasant? Because the issue or issues weren't resolved? Maybe because of both factors—the process and the
results?

We hope you know when you experience the pain of damaging conflicts. Some people don't seem to realize when
they're in pain. Usually it's because they have trouble admit-
ting everything isn't perfect, or at least satisfactory. If they

did, they would have to acknowledge that they aren't in full control of their lives. When you ask them, "How're you doing?" they invariably reply, "Fine" or "OK."

Some people simply lack the understanding and words to communicate their pain to anyone else. Not only are they unable to tell you or God where they're hurting, but they're unable to even detect their pain and communicate it to themselves. If we've just described you, take heart! You can learn these skills. We encourage you to consult with someone who specializes in assisting people identify feelings—a pastor, counselor, or medical doctor, for example.

If you know that you're hurting from a painful conflict, we encourage you to set out on a journey of healing. That journey will ususally take time. Don't rush it, but don't put it off indefinitely. Here are some suggestions for acknowledging the pain and starting to cure it:

- Identify where in your body the physical pain resides.
- Describe the pain to yourself and perhaps to a trustworthy confidante. ("My stomach's tense and upset.")
- Recognize, label, and express (both privately and publicly, if possible) one or more feelings you believe are connected to your painful physical sensations. ("I didn't realize just how much I let that conflict hurt me! I'm sad about how it turned out. And irritated too.")
- Admit that those are some of your feelings and accept them. ("Yes, I'm hurt and sad. That's OK to feel too. It sure doesn't make me weak.")
- Decide what produced your feelings (the negotiation process, result, or both) and why your pain is so intense. ("What bothers me most is that I wasn't able to change her mind. It really bugs me that I can't have more influence over someone.")
- Choose whether or not you want to end the pain. ("I need some time to grieve about this" or "I want a 'pity party.' I don't want to let go of the hurt and resentment I'm feeling right now. Maybe later!" or "I'm now ready to get rid of this pain.")
- Ask God for strength and guidance either to continue with the healing or to prepare you to be more willing to

cure the pain which you face.

Healing Method 2: Valuing the Restorative Effects of Forgiveness

We're convinced that the most effective and lasting way to heal the pain of damaging conflicts is through forgiveness—forgiving and, if possible, being forgiven. There are a number of thoughtful self-help books with a Christian orientation on this topic. We recommend some sources in case you want to study this topic further. Two are written by David Augsburger, to whom we refer several times in this book. They are *The Freedom of Forgiveness* (1970) and *Caring Enough to Forgive and Caring Enough to Not Forgive* (1981). Two other good books are *Forgive, Forget, and Be Free* (1981) by Jeanette Lockerbie and *Forgive and Forget: Healing the Hurts We Don't Deserve* (1984) by Lewis Smedes.

It's easy to assume that no one disagrees with the effective use of forgiveness. But beware! Not everyone gets excited about forgiveness as an antidote to emotional (and related physical) pain. Some people believe they don't have the right or freedom to forgive anyone. They don't believe any human is in a position to bestow forgiveness on another. Furthermore, many individuals don't accept the concept or principles of God's forgiveness. They ignore what the Bible says on this topic.

We recommend that, if for no other reason, you value the power of human forgiveness because God has commanded us to do it. That's sufficient reason for us! Many passages of Scripture address forgiveness. Both the Old and New Testaments exhort their readers to turn the other cheek. Look at these for additional encouragement:

- Then Peter came and said to Him, "Lord, how often shall my brother sin against me and I forgive him? Up to seven times?" Jesus said to him, "I do not say to you, up to seven times, but up to seventy times seven" (Matt. 18:21-22).
- For if you forgive men for their transgressions, your Heavenly Father will also forgive you. But if you do not

forgive men, then your Father will not forgive your transgressions (Matt. 6:14-15).

■ Bless those who persecute you; bless and curse not. Do not be overcome by evil, but overcome evil with good (Rom. 12:14, 21).

■ He who conceals his transgressions will not prosper, but he who confesses and forsakes them will find compassion (Prov. 28:13).

We predict that if you're like the two of us, even with the clear biblical message addressed by these verses, forgiveness won't always come easily. It's hard to forgive someone who is abusive or spiteful to you. It's even more difficult to forgive someone who doesn't care whether or not he or she is forgiven. There are also those who won't accept your apology for what you contributed to a conflict.

If you're struggling to get excited about forgiveness even after prayerful study of biblical imperatives, try three additional ideas. First, list the benefits of forgiveness that appeal to you. Smedes addresses the topic, "Why Forgive?" He advances the following benefits of forgiveness:

■ "... because forgiving is the only way we have to a better fairness in our unfair world..." (p. 124).

■ "Forgiving is the *only* way to be fair to yourself" (p. 132).

■ "Forgiving comes equipped with the toughness of realism.... Only realists can be forgivers.... Forgiving begins with the power to shake off deception and deal with reality" (p. 141).

■ "You forgive in freedom and then move on to greater freedom. Freedom is strength; you know you have it when you have the power to forgive" (p. 143).

■ "Love is the power behind forgiveness.... Love does not make us pushovers for people who hurt us unfairly. Love forgives, but only because love is powerful" (p. 143).

■ "Forgiving fits faulty folk. And we are all faulty" (p. 149).

If your "benefits analysis" doesn't cement your commitment to forgiveness, consider another idea. Make a conscious decision to proceed with forgiveness anyway. Then try experimenting. Start the forgiveness process with someone with whom you've had a painful conflict. The next three methods suggest some steps to take. You might like what happens as a result.

Healing Method 3: Seeking Forgiveness from Opponents

When a conflict goes sour and feelings are hurt, most of us wait, hoping our adversary will come to his senses, admit how he botched the negotiations, and apologize with sincerity. Though this is what most of us would like, the Bible establishes a different standard.

Jesus said you should leave your time of worship when you "remember that your brother has something against you" and "first be reconciled to your brother" (Matt. 5:23-24). According to Jesus, true worship cannot occur where conflict is present. That means you're challenged to *begin the reconciliation.*

You won't get far starting with an accusatory statement, such as: "You blew it, I'm hurt, and I want an apology." You'll be much more effective if you initiate that discussion by confessing your contribution to the damaging conflict. *Accept some of the responsibility—even if your only contribution consists of the distance you've allowed to grow between the two of you—and request your opponent's forgiveness for it.* That tact could be very disarming as well as pleasing to your adversary.

Here are some suggestions for seeking forgiveness from your opponent:

- Ask God for strength and guidance.
- Pray that God will prepare your opponent's mind and feelings.
- Agree to a mutually acceptable time and place to meet to discuss the damaging conflict.
- Prepare for the meeting by recalling what you did to cause the problem, and decide if you're truly sorry for it.
- Then, most important of all, repent of what you did. Repent literally means to "change your thinking" and reorient your mind. Turn off the old "mental tapes" that led to the initial problem. Then, act accordingly, in ways

that please God, yourself, and your adversary. Think of what you might do to make up for your initial action. In the actual meeting, try the following:

- Listen carefully and quietly to the other person, while trying to see the situation from her perspective.
- Don't tell the person, "You shouldn't feel that way." Feelings are never wrong or inappropriate.
- Don't apologize too hastily. If you do, you'll seem insincere and unaware of how seriously your opponent perceives the situation.
- Sincerely ask for forgiveness and demonstrate the fruits of repentance by revealing your "new mind" in word and deed.

This is an important moment in the meeting. Don't rush your opponent. Wait for a response, and be prepared for a possible refusal. If your opponent is receptive and seems willing to accept your apology, continue with the following:

- Ask if there is anything you can do to make up for the wrong. If there is, agree with the request, if you possibly can.
- Promise not to do the action again in the future (true repentance).
- Express appreciation to the other party.

Finally, don't forget these crucial steps:

- Thank God for His help in this forgiving process.
- Repattern your life, if necessary, to reduce future hurts from damaging conflicts.

At this point, you'll be well prepared to forgive your opponent—*whether or not you are apologized to.* In case your opponent does seek forgiveness from you, check the next method for some ways to proceed.

Healing Method 4: Forgiving Opponents for Damaging Conflicts

We hope you'll encounter some opponents who, like you, want forgiveness for what they contributed to the damage.

The effectiveness of Methods 3 and 4 depends on several conditions. First, you must be convinced that forgiveness (giving and receiving it) is necessary to cure the hurt of damaging conflicts. Second, you must be capable of taking the necessary time to repent and seek forgiveness and to take the specific steps to bestow it. Too many of us make the mistake of rushing through the forgiving process and grossly simplifying it.

Third, you should know *what forgiveness is not.* For example, we agree with Smedes that it isn't looking the other way; making light of a destructive action; trying to maintain a peaceful coexistence at all costs; being excessively tolerant; or attempting to fade memories without first forgiving.

We trust that some of these suggestions will make it easier for you to forgive others.

- Ask God to prepare your mind and feelings for genuine forgiveness. Also ask Him to guide the other person.
- Try to determine your opponent's possible reasons and perspective for his or her hurtful actions.
- Accept (even if you don't approve of) that perspective.
- Decide what you'd like to have from your opponent at this point, yet proceed with the decision to forgive even if you don't receive what you'd like.
- Plan what you'd like to say. Write it out and practice it.
- Agree to a mutually acceptable time and place to meet to discuss the damaging conflict.

Once the two of you get together, try the following:

- Ask the person to forgive you for your part.
- Share your feelings, the impact of the hurtful event, your desire to forgive, and what you would like from the other person (for example, accepting responsibility for the hurtful action).
- If offered, accept his or her apology for wrongdoing.
- Don't take an apology lightly. ("Oh, that was nothing.") Instead, be sincere and sensitive in listening to and accepting his or her statement.
- State any request you may want the other person to do.
- Express appreciation to your opponent.

Before you end the process:

- Determine at least one thing you've learned from this conflict that will make it easier for you in future ones.

■ Accept the possibility that your forgiveness journey may not happen quickly. If you haven't dealt with everything within yourself, complete forgiveness might not occur until later. You may not be able to forgive "right now."

■ Remember to thank God for His help and guidance.

Realize that most pain from damaging conflicts won't end when forgiveness and reconciliation occur. This final condition requires Method 5—doing something about painful memories.

Healing Method 5: Fading the Memories of Damaging Conflicts

Forgive and forget! That's a typical challenge verbalized by combatants struggling to reconcile. Not only that, it's part of the title of several well-conceived books on forgiveness. Though this is a trend, we can't agree with it.

Most memories of damaging conflicts are difficult, if not impossible to forget entirely. If you accept the challenge to eliminate something from your memory bank, you're in for a rigorous test unless God performs a miracle. We recommend that you concentrate instead on *fading those memories.* In that way, they'll become less and less frequent and eventually lose their power over you. Here are five suggestions for how to fade painful memories:

1. *Lower the intensity* of the feelings you attach to those memories. As time passes following the damaging conflict, you'll usually (not always) feel less intense about it. But such "emotional defusing" invariably takes action, not just the passage of time. Prayer and forgiveness are the most powerful actions we know for defusing such feelings. Also, make a conscious decision to feel "mildly" about the conflict and your opponent. You'll find this level of feeling easier to live with than one of intensity.

2. Try *stopping thoughts.* Picture a red light when you start to think a counterproductive thought associated with the painful memory. Or yell "Stop!" to yourself.

A sudden, positive change in your posture might be another way to "arrest" painful ideas.

3. Work on *replacing thoughts.* Replace a disturbing thought with a more constructive one. Substitute a pleasant scene (ocean beach, spring skiing) or a logical, truthful sentence. ("I learned a lot from that conflict; I'll do much better next time.")

4. Engage in *incompatible behavior.* Do something that makes it impossible for you to think about an unpleasant memory and feel its related emotions. Riding his horse does this for Brian. It's impossible for him to stay on his horse and ruminate on damaging conflicts at the same time!

5. *Repattern your life.* Change any of your behaviors that contributed to your role in the painful conflict. This is the ultimate test of authentic repentance. Here you have a reason to grow. Seize this moment of opportunity!

By experimenting with techniques such as these, you'll be able to recall unpleasant conflicts without ending up in intense emotional states. You'll be more constructively detached as you unhook your emotional connections to these memories.

Restored for a Purpose
By healing the damage of badly resolved conflicts, our hope is that you'll progress further than just resolving those disagreements. We recommend that your *immediate* goal in the healing process be to restore relationships: with God (if the conflicts create distance between you and Him) and your opponents (if they're willing to reunite with you).

You may even have to restore your "relationship with yourself." By that we mean learning to accept and like yourself for who you are. With God's help, you can overcome self-doubt and go on to become the kind of fully-developed person He designed you to be.

At the same time, consider setting this as your ultimate goal: *to consistently use the Better End Strategy in conflict resolution.* That requires your commitment to assert with respect, confront with care, demonstrate strength laced with tenderness, and show firmness mingled with love. Paul's exhortation to the Corinthians captures this goal, "Be on the alert, stand firm in the faith, act like men, be strong. Let all that you do be done in love" (1 Cor. 16:13-14). We offer some final thoughts on that challenge in the following chapter. Now, to help you heal any damaging conflicts from your present and past, complete the following experiments. We think they'll help you to heal the hurt and close important doors.

Experiment 19: "Self-Assessment of a Painful Conflict"

For this experiment, choose a recent conflict that created pain for you at the time—and perhaps still does.
A. Answer each of the following questions about this conflict:
1. What actually happened? (What did each of you do at the time?)

2. What made the conflict painful?

3. Specifically, how have you handled your hurt up to now?

4. Looking back, how do you wish you had handled that conflict?

5. What do you think you might to do handle any remaining pain or unresolved issues?

6. Which of our five suggestions could help you fade the painful memories of that conflict?

7. What could you do about painful conflicts that arise in the future (with this person or with others)?

B. Discuss your responses with someone else making progress in conflict resolution skills.

Experiment 20: "Personal Forgiveness Plan"

A. Select a conflict that resulted in pain or bitterness. It could be the one you used in Experiment 19 or another unresolved situation.

B. Answer the following questions about this conflict.
   1. Where are you now in the forgiveness process?

   2. What do you need to do next to move ahead toward healing?

   3. What's one goal you agree to reach regarding this painful conflict?

   4. Specifically, what is one forgiveness step you commit to take?

   5. By what date will you take that step?

C. Review your forgiveness plan with someone who not only cares about you but who's also a skilled conflict-resolver.

CHAPTER ELEVEN

Being an Agreeable Person—without Being a Wimp

The wicked flee when no one is pursuing, but the righteous are bold as a lion.

—*Proverbs 28:1*

In this last chapter, we have three final ideas for you to consider. First, we want to address a fear you might have. "If I adopt the fair and principled approach you recommend, will I be labeled a wimp?" Second, we'll discuss the *inner qualities* of Better End conflict-resolvers— what's beyond the outward skills and behaviors they use in conflicts. Finally, we want to help you with an action plan for handling future conflicts in your life.

Wimps vs. BEST Negotiators
Most people are turned off by the image of a wimp, even if it's not universally agreed on what it means to be one. Prob-

ably each person who uses that label defines it differently. To us, "wimp" signifies someone who is too nice, giving to a fault, and too anxious to please.

Unfortunately, some people fear that the ideal negotiators we describe in this book will be viewed as wimps. They reject the Better End Strategy, concerned they'll be seen by others as weaklings.

If this is your view, you're missing the major thrust of our message. You and these other critics are equating our model negotiators to the *avoiders* (ostriches) and *accommodators* (doves) we describe in chapter 3.

BEST negotiators are definitely not wimps! Here are some major differences that we see between wimps and them.

Wimps, as a rule:

- give in automatically on issues;
- always put other people first, trying to please everybody;
- are very self-effacing, constantly putting themselves down (because of this, they're very difficult to be around for long);
- don't know what they want or don't want, or what they care deeply about (therefore, they're easily swayed and talked into things);
- are frequently taken unfair advantage of.

No wonder people don't want to be in this category when wimp is defined this way.

On the other hand, *BEST negotiators:*

- seek truth even when the process takes time;
- sometimes give in—willingly and purposely—on issues, yet more often they do not. (Instead, they hang in there with opponents to find creative solutions which will please both sides);
- consider other persons the same as themselves—no better and no worse—and have no reason or desire to put down themselves;
- know what they believe in, value, and want because they actively seek God's direction for their lives;
- swallow their pride, admit their mistakes, and change their minds when they see a better way of doing things;
- are almost never taken unfair advantage of;

■ are respected, sought out, and valued as friends and professional associates.

No one even thinks of calling them wimps. Like Christ, they're an integrated combination of tough and tender, firm yet soft, and strong but humble.

So, forget any fear about being called a wimp as you strategize in resolving conflicts. God can help you be bold as a lion or tender as a lamb—at the same time, in the same circumstance. You'll soon wonder why you ever settled for anything less.

The Inner Qualities of BEST Negotiators

We've presented many skills, how-to ideas, and experiments in this book. Our fear is that our recommended approaches might sound mechanistic to you. Some individuals may read the book, learn some or even all of the techniques, and still miss our point.

The Better End Strategy is much more than steps or formulas. It's more than externally observable actions. BEST negotiators possess (or are striving to develop) certain inner qualities and attitudes. For example, they:

■ possess courage. They aren't afraid to challenge tough issues and go face-to-face with adversaries, even the more difficult ones.

■ feel deep concern for what's true, right, and just in human interactions. They refuse to go along with popular opinions or trends when these are wrong. Their main source of truth is God's Word.

■ are sensitive and tender toward the other person's feelings, needs, and wants. They always try to be hard on issues and soft on people's hearts.

■ demonstrate sincere appreciation for the skills God has allowed them to develop and the accomplishments they have experienced. They always give credit to the Lord for His guidance and direction.

Life Goals for BEST Negotiators

If you have the goal of consistently using the Better End Strategy, you have your work cut out for you. Accomplishing that goal will require a lifelong process of developing godly character and practicing resolution skills. No one is a born negotiator.

Successful conflict-resolvers have worked for years to refine and polish their skills and to develop their related inner qualities. They allow God to mold them and smooth the rough edges that inevitably emerge. We're excited to be "in process" and invite you to join us on this journey.

As you think about potential goals for yourself, here are some reminders of the core of the Better End Strategy. The approach is based on three biblical principles:

■ *Pursuing peace* with others (Heb. 12:14; Mark 9:50; John 20:19);
■ *Valuing interdependence*—doing what's good for each other (1 Thes. 5:15);
■ *Using wisdom and reason*—with God as part of the planning—in negotiations (James 3:17).

Using this approach that we've found so helpful, you'll try to accomplish outcomes such as these (the BEST in a nutshell):

■ Seek God's wisdom before you act.
■ Approach conflict negotiation as a potentially enjoyable experience.
■ Resolve minor disagreements before they become major conflicts.
■ Discuss points where you and your opponent agree be fore concentrating on issues of disagreement.
■ Emphasize collaboration in your conflict resolution sessions, and deemphasize unconditional surrender (yours or theirs).
■ Reaffirm regularly your commitment to please God and eliminate any inclination to compromise biblical principles.
■ Have options when impasses and deadlocks arise.
■ Know fair and principled ways of responding to any unfair tactics of your adversaries.

- Initiate the healing-forgiveness process when damaging conflicts occur.
- Make restitution to opponents you have wronged in damaging conflicts.
- Assess and polish (on an ongoing basis) the quality of your negotiating performance.

In assessing your negotiating skills and inner qualities, ask yourself questions such as these before you respond: "Will I glorify God if I act this way?" "What words might Jesus use to respond to this person?"

Such questions and the BEST answers to them provide the type of restraint all of us need if we want to settle disagreements constructively. In fact, that brings us full circle to Jesus' teaching, "Blessed are the meek," with which we began this book.

We're convinced that He wasn't giving preferential treatment to the weak and passive! The word "meek," which Jesus used, refers elsewhere to the bridling of a high-spirited horse. The spirit of the person, then, is not shattered, destroyed, or walked on. It's simply bridled—channeled in the right direction.

God wants our spirits to be under His control. In all of our actions we are to be under this rein of the Lord. Asking and responding to "bridling" questions can help you and us be more God-directed and centered.

We encourage you to test out these ideas a few at a time. You won't master this book or this strategy in one reading, but you've taken an important step by getting this far.

Before you close the book, write out your action plan for *one change* you'd like to make related to conflict resolution. The plan should help you keep your sights on better ends in the coming weeks and months.

We'd like to know how the process goes for you. Write us (c/o Victor Books, P.O. Box 1825, Wheaton, Illinois 60189) and tell us of your struggles and successes. Though we might not be able to respond to all your individual letters, we'll use your wisdom to improve our message to future readers and negotiators we train. Thanks for your help!

Experiment 21: "My Wimp Image"
For this experiment, consider how you (and others) view
your "wimp image."
A. Answer the questions below with candor.
  1. Have you ever considered yourself a wimp? If so,
      what were the circumstances? If not, why not?

  2. Has anyone else ever directly or indirectly called
      you a wimp? Describe the situation.

  3. What emotions do you feel at the thought of being a
      wimp?

  4. As a result of studying this book, what would you
      like to do about your "wimp image"?

B. Discuss your responses with someone you trust.

Experiment 22: "My Conflict Resolution Plan"
Use this form to set a goal and plan your own action strategy for handling conflicts over the next six months.
A. Write down a few words for each of the following:
  1. One conflict-related goal I want to accomplish:

  2. One obstacle I may encounter on my way to this
      goal:

  3. Two things I can do to get around this obstacle:
      a.
      b.

  4. To celebrate reaching my goal, I'll:

  5. Think beyond the next six months, how could you
      improve your character as a conflict-resolver?

B. Discuss your plan with a trusted friend who can encour-
    age you and hold you accountable.

Checklist for the Better End Strategy

The following is a summary—in checklist form—of the Better End Strategy (BEST). Use it as you prepare for and carry out conflict resolution meetings. Not all conflicts and negotiations will require every step or feature of the strategy, so select the parts that are appropriate for the situation you face.

Preparing to Resolve the Conflict

I'LL GATHER THE FOLLOWING INFORMATION ON MYSELF:

_____ How biblical principles relate to this conflict
_____ What I see as causes of the conflict
_____ Key issue(s) to be resolved
_____ My feelings about the other party and the issue(s)
_____ Alternatives I see (at this point) for resolving the conflict
_____ My Best Alternative to a Negotiated Agreement (BATNA) with the other party

_____ My sense of God's will for resolution of this conflict

I'LL GATHER THE FOLLOWING INFORMATION ON THE OTHER PARTY:

_____ Probable feelings toward me and the issue(s)
_____ Probable goals or desired outcomes of this negotiation
_____ His or her BATNA
_____ Typical style in handling conflicts such as this

IN PLANNING THE LOGISTICS OF THE MEETING, I'LL:

_____ Note possible times and places we could meet
_____ Plan what to say in inviting the other person to meet
_____ Decide how to extend the invitation (by phone, in person, in writing)

TO COMPLETE THIS PLANNING, I'LL ALSO:

_____ Pray about the conflict and its resolution
_____ Picture myself handling the meeting successfully
_____ Practice the meeting with someone who can give me constructive suggestions on my points and approach

Conducting the Conflict Resolution Meeting

AS I PARTICIPATE IN THE MEETING, I'LL:

_____ Set a positive tone by remarking that my goal is mutual agreement and satisfaction
_____ Decide whether a formal or informal agenda (list of issues, in order) is appropriate
_____ Set up the agenda
_____ Set up ground rules for the discussion
_____ Determine physical signals to use (if appropriate)
_____ Establish a procedure for taking time-outs
_____ Use active listening to understand other person's views, needs, and feelings

_____ Keep track of my own feelings, needs, and goals

_____ Take regular body and feelings checks to note my reactions, and then adjust my actions accordingly

_____ Address each issue, one by one, until resolved (or postponed)

_____ Take turns expressing feelings, concerns, needs, and desired outcomes on each issue

_____ Propose and discuss possible solutions for each issue

_____ Expand the "pie" of possible solutions and benefits so both of us can meet our needs

_____ Agree on one of the alternatives and jot down what we agreed

_____ Make a positive comment about each issue resolved and express appreciation to other party

_____ Review the meeting part way, and take stock of my performance

_____ Take "process checks" to see if both of us are comfortable with the way the meeting is going

_____ Reaffirm my need for God's guidance throughout this conflict

_____ Make appealing proposals to the other side

_____ Handle objections to my ideas

_____ Handle personal attacks on me without getting defensive

_____ Avoid bringing up old issues at inappropriate times

_____ Reframe criticisms or attacks on me as attacks on the problem

TO OVERCOME IMPASSES, I'LL:

_____ Assume this is an impasse (and not an unresolvable deadlock)

_____ Summarize the dilemma, as I see it, and get agreement on what the impasse is about

_____ Reframe the dilemma as a search for a new, better solution

_____ Probe for hidden needs and issues

_____ If appropriate, submit with pleasure to the solution proposed by the other party

_____ Agree to accept part of the other party's solution(s)
_____ Agree to try the solution on a trial basis

ON APPARENT DEADLOCKS, I'LL:

_____ Use *incubation* (committing the conflict to God and waiting)
_____ Use *adaptation* (accepting my difficult opponent as he or she is, adapting my behavior, withdrawing as needed, refusing to negotiate again until opponent has made progress)
_____ Use structured *separation*—only if both of us explicitly agree
_____ Use *mediation* (third party) in negotiations
_____ Use *arbitration* (a more structured process with a third-party decision)

WHEN DEALING WITH UNFAIR, UNPRINCIPLED OPPONENTS, I'LL:

_____ Recognize unfair tactics throughout the negotiation process
_____ Use fair and principled countertactics in response to unfair moves

TO CLOSE THE NEGOTIATION MEETING, I'LL:

_____ Determine who is responsible for implementing each part of the settlement
_____ Set dates by which tasks are to be started and/or finished
_____ Decide how we'll monitor the implementation
_____ Determine rewards for completing tasks
_____ Determine consequences for not completing tasks
_____ Set date for reviewing the agreement(s)
_____ Write draft copy of our agreement(s)
_____ End the resolution meeting on a positive note by expressing appreciation to the other side and stressing the shared benefits

_____ Pray together or alone, as appropriate, thanking God for His help throughout the process

_____ Use appropriate form of physical touch (handshake, hug) to close

Following Up after the Meeting

TO FOLLOW UP LATER, I'LL:

_____ Finalize our written agreement

_____ Get copies of the written agreement to both sides

_____ Follow through on tasks to which I've agreed

_____ Take time by myself to evaluate the negotiation meeting

_____ As appropriate, meet or talk with the other side to discuss how we handled the negotiation

_____ Drop him or her an informal note to express appreciation

_____ Monitor our agreement(s) as planned

_____ Mention any deviations before they become large

_____ Set up another meeting if all issues aren't resolved to satisfaction

_____ Ask God to continue to help me with this relationship and with the handling of the situation

_____ Review what I've learned that will help me improve future conflict resolutions

Special Applications for Group Conflicts

_____ Decide whether and how to use a conflict resolution team

_____ Design and conduct a large-group conflict resolution session

_____ Use the one-text procedure to get agreement from participants

RESOURCES

Augsburger, David. *The Freedom of Forgiveness.* Chicago: Moody Press, 1970.

————. *Caring Enough to Confront.* Ventura, Calif.: Regal Books, 1981.

————. *Caring Enough to Forgive and Caring Enough to Not Forgive.* Ventura, Calif.: Regal Books, 1981.

Bazerman, Max H. "Why Negotiations Go Wrong." *Psychology Today,* June 1986, pp. 54–58.

Bramson, Robert. *Difficult People*. New York: Ballantine, 1981.

Chapman, Gary. *Hope for the Separated*. Chicago: Moody Press, 1982.

Christian Conciliation Service, P.O. Box 2069, Oak Park, Illinois 60303, Phone: (312) 848-7735.

Cohen, Herb. *You Can Negotiate Anything*. Secaucus, N.J.: Lyle Stuart Inc., 1980.

Dawson, Roger. *You Can Get Anything You Want (But You Have to Do More than Ask)*. New York: Regency Books, 1985.

Douglas, J.D., ed. *The New Bible Dictionary*. Grand Rapids: William B. Eerdmans, 1962.

Elgin, Suzette Haden. *The Gentle Art of Verbal Self-Defense*. Englewood Cliffs, N.J.: Prentice Hall, 1987.

Fisher, Roger and Ury, William. *Getting to Yes: Negotiating without Giving In*. New York: Penguin Books, 1983.

Jones, G. Brian and Phillips-Jones, Linda. *Men Have Feelings, Too!* Wheaton, Ill.: Victor Books, 1988.

Kipnis, David and Schmidt, Stuart. "The Language of Persuasion." *Psychology Today*. April 1985, pp. 40–45.

Landorf, Joyce. *Irregular People*. Waco, Texas: Word Books, 1982.

Lockerbie, Jeanette. *Forgive, Forget and Be Free*. Chappaqua, N.Y.: Christian Herald Books, 1981.

Mace, David R. "Resolving Conflict in Marriage." *Christian Home*. Fall 1985, pp. 56–60.

Nierenberg, G.I. *The Art of Negotiating*. New York: E.P. Dutton, 1968.

Seamands, David. *Healing for Damaged Emotions*. Wheaton, Ill.: Victor Books, 1981.

Smedes, Lewis B. *Forgive and Forget: Healing the Hurts We Don't Deserve.* San Francisco: Harper and Row, 1984.

Vuchinich, Samuel. "Arguments, Family Style." *Psychology Today.* October 1985, pp. 40–46.

NOTES

NOTES